Santa and the Scribes:
The Making of Fort Kochi

Santa and the Scribes: The Making of Fort Kochi

| Sketches & Text |

E.P. UNNY

NIYOGI
BOOKS

Published by

NIYOGI BOOKS

D-78, Okhla Industrial Area, Phase-I
New Delhi-110 020, INDIA
Tel: 91-11-26816301, 49327000
Fax: 91-11-26810483, 26813830
Email: niyogibooks@gmail.com
Website: www.niyogibooksindia.com

Editor: Jayalakshmi Sengupta
Design: Misha Oberoi

ISBN: 978-93-83098-35-4
Year of Publication: 2014
Reprint: 2023

Printed at: Niyogi Offset Pvt. Ltd., New Delhi, India

To

E.B. Unni and Rajalakshmi Unni

—my uncle and aunt

who made Fort Kochi their home

Dedication: Aspinwall & Company, one of the corporate landmarks of Fort Kochi
Epigraph: Riverside view of Fort Kochi from Vypin island
Contents: A vantage view of Fort Kochi and the harbour from Cochin Port Trust Chairman's office
Kochi Timeline: The islands off Fort Kochi and the mainland of Ernakulam

CALVIN: Our country was founded a very long time ago, roughly around 200 B.C.

TEACHER: 200 B.C.?!

CALVIN: Before Calvin. That's what's important!

—Calvin and Hobbes Bill Watterson

Contents

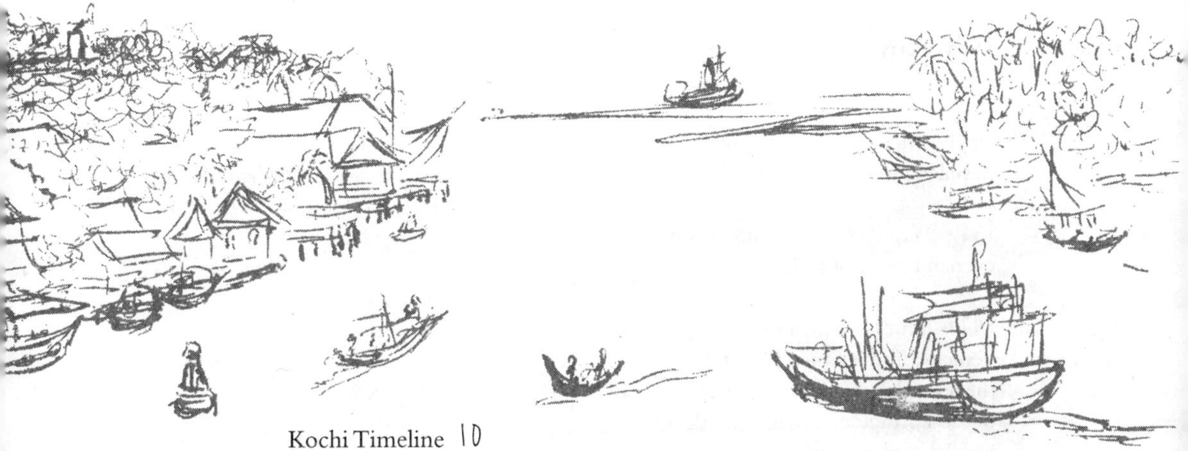

Kochi Timeline 10
Kochi Map 12

A Journey through Chronicles 15
Little Lisbon 61
Homely Holland 101
Mini England 127
Karl Marx, Other Jews and the Like 173

Bibliography 212
Acknowledgements 215

Kochi Timeline

1341 Periyar River floods to desilt and create a navigable harbour at Kochi.

1440 Niccolò de' Conti, an Italian traveller, reaches Kochi overland.

1487 Pêro da Covilhã embarks on overland recce of Indian spice trade.

1497 John Cabbot, a merchant from Venice commissioned by England and the legendary Vasco da Gama, the envoy of the Portugese crown, embark on parallel explorations.

1498 Vasco da Gama completes historic voyage at Kozhikode on the Malabar Coast.

1500 Pedro Álvares Cabral lands at Kochi.

1500 Portugal privatises its monopoly sea route to India.

1502 Vasco da Gama reaches Malabar Coast on his second voyage—marked by atrocities against Muslims in Kozhikode and relative tact in Kochi.

1503 Rajah of Kochi permits the Portuguese to build a fort in Kochi.

1504 Duarte Pacheco fights a five month long battle against the Samudri to establish Portuguese foothold in Kochi.

1509 Afonso de Albuquerque takes over as Governor of Kochi.

1524 Vasco da Gama back in Kochi as Viceroy in early November and dies here on Christmas Eve.

1548 Francis Xavier reaches Kochi.

1585 The cumbersome tri-partite trade pact, the Portuguese inked in with merchants and the native state of Kochi.

1662 The fleeing Portuguese raze down Jew Town.

1663 The Dutch capture Kochi.

1673–1677 Van Rheede served as Dutch Governor of Kochi and commissioned *Hortus Malabaricus*, the classic treatise on Malabar's plant life.

1719 The idol of Thirumala Devaswom Temple vanishes.

1741 Historic battle won against a European power on the Indian coast by Travancore maharaja, Marthanda Varma who defeated Dutch Commander De Lannoy.

1791 Sakthan Thampuran Rama Varma raids Kochi bazaar.

1803 The British demolish the last of Kochi's three forts built by the Dutch.

1806 Much of Dutch Kochi destroyed by the British.

1808 Colonel Colin Macaulay, the first British Resident of Kochi, forced to flee through an underground tunnel.

1808 Koder family comes to Kochi.

1814 Anglo-Dutch Treaty signed by the British, cede island of Banca to the Dutch in exchange for Kochi.

1826 Rev. Samuel Ridsdale arrives in Kochi from Kottayam.

1835 Rev. Ridsdale converts a Kochi prince and his companion at the St. Francis Church.

1859 The British government in Madras rules in favour of Kochi in the dispute over the idol of Thirumala Devaswom Temple.

1860 William Brunton starts Kochi's first newspaper, *Cochin Argus*.

1920 Robert Bristow arrives in Kochi.

1947 India wins freedom from British rule and Fort Kochi from over four centuries of European dominance.

1948 Israel becomes a nation and Kochi's Jews start looking towards their homeland.

1956 The linguistic state of Kerala is formed, with Kochi as part of it.

1957 Kerala elects a Communist government.

1981 Kochi's legendary singer Mehboob dies.

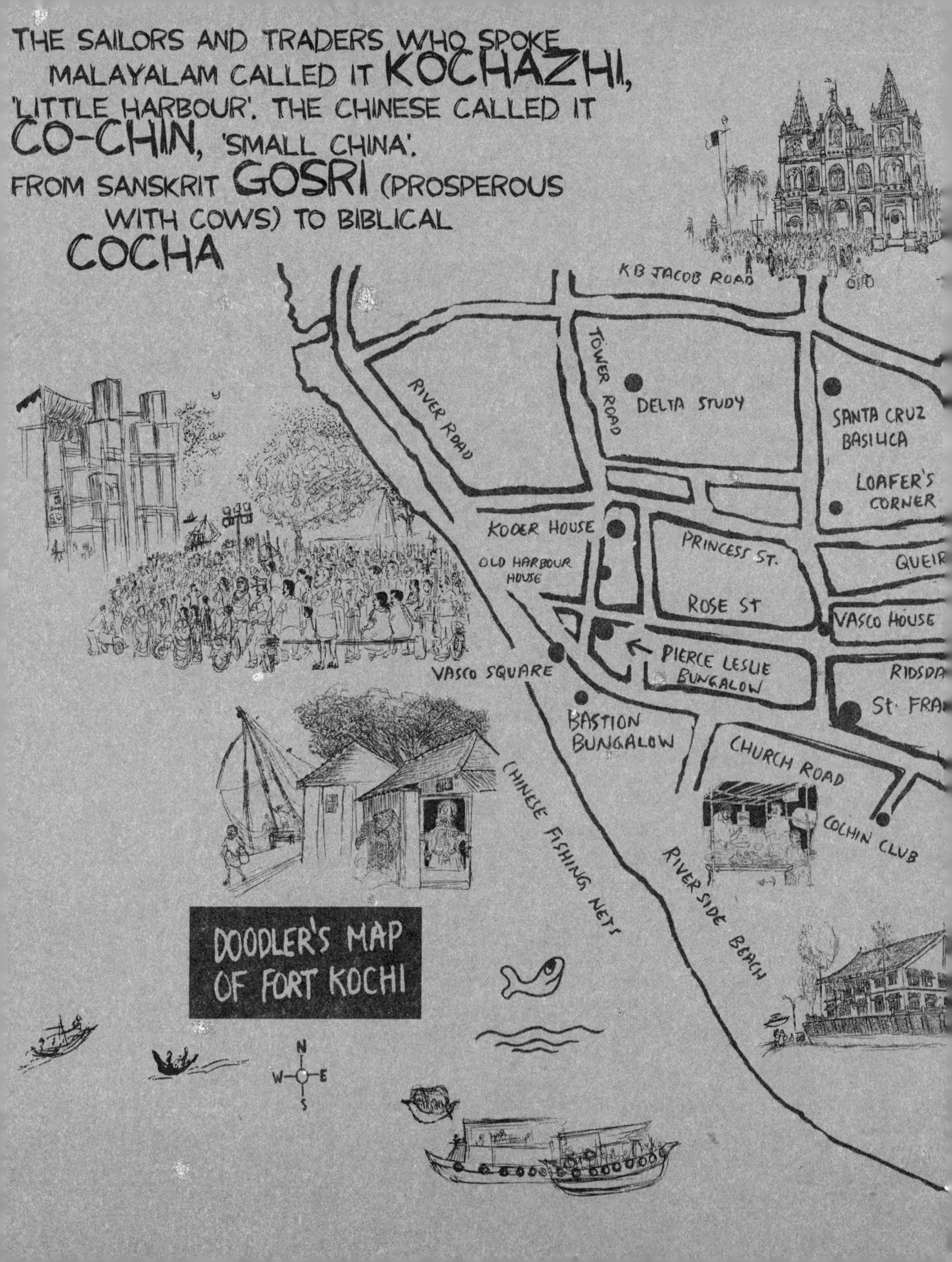
THE SAILORS AND TRADERS WHO SPOKE MALAYALAM CALLED IT KOCHAZHI, 'LITTLE HARBOUR'. THE CHINESE CALLED IT CO-CHIN, 'SMALL CHINA'. FROM SANSKRIT GOSRI (PROSPEROUS WITH COWS) TO BIBLICAL COCHA
KB JACOB ROAD
TOWER ROAD
RIVER ROAD
DELTA STUDY
SANTA CRUZ BASILICA
LOAFER'S CORNER
KODER HOUSE
PRINCESS ST.
QUEIR
OLD HARBOUR HOUSE
ROSE ST
VASCO HOUSE
PIERCE LESLIE BUNGALOW
RIDSDA
VASCO SQUARE
St. FRA
BASTION BUNGALOW
CHURCH ROAD
CHINESE FISHING NETS
COCHIN CLUB
RIVER SIDE BEACH
DOODLER'S MAP OF FORT KOCHI
N
W
E
S

IN SIXTEENTH AND SEVENTEENTH CENTURIES, EUROPEAN TONGUES FOUND AMENABLE VARIATIONS—**COCYM, COCHYM, COCHIN, COCHI ...**

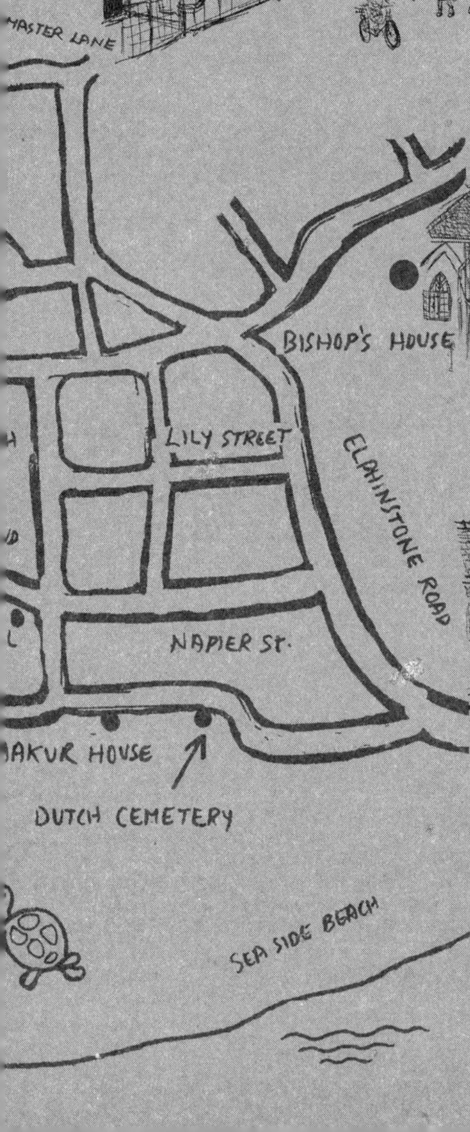

TO THE PORTUGUESE KOCHI BECAME **'LITTLE LISBON'**, TO THE DUTCH **'HOMELY HOLLAND'** AND TO THE ENGLISH **'MINI ENGLAND'.**

A Journey Through Chronicles

The jangar that transports commuters and vehicles between Fort Kochi and Vypin

A street corner

An European colony for 444 years, home to Muslims and Jews for longer. A sixteenth century cathedral, an older church, vintage trading houses, a 150-year-old Chamber of Commerce, a five-month-long battle, four historic transfers of power, three forts built and demolished, fourteen languages, Vasco da Gama, Pedro Álvares Cabral, St. Francis Xavier, Hendrik van Rheede, Sir Robert Bristow ...

Pack all of this and a million mosquitoes into one square mile and you have Fort Kochi—a fishing village on the south-western coast of India that zoomed into the world map as trade town and fortified colonial capital, now a fort-less global tourist destination. Also, arguably, the most written about town in India, thanks to sustained European presence over the years.

Few spots in Asia can claim such density of diverse European experience, swears the tourist guide.

In a forenoon the guide conducts you through nineteen declared heritage sites.

It is heritage tourism that drives Fort Kochi, and no longer fishing, spice trade or tea auctions.

The occasional fisherman trying his luck. In the background is the Cochin Port Trust Office on Willingdon Island

Fishermen are still around and they work the same old way, only, their row boats are motorised and their nets synthetic. They fish because fish breed in water.

Fishermen readying for another foray

Aspinwall & Company, one of the corporate landmarks of Fort Kochi

On land, vocations have changed drastically. Trading houses are moving out to make way for the hospitality sector.

Mercantile Kochi's big brands like Peirce Leslie and Aspinwall will fade out of here unless the new buyers choose to keep the names for old time's sake.

This is how another big name in the commercial annals of Kochi, Brunton Boatyard, has survived. The boatyard, long in disuse, is now a landmark heritage hotel on the waterfront.

Yoga at the waterfront. Brunton Boatyard Hotel

An old street house partly renovated as homestay for tourists on Napier Street

Nearly every roofed structure, barring temples, churches, mosques and monuments is ready to house visitors, either as full-scale resorts or as homestays.

Any spot with a water view is a sure grab. Not just for the sake of the much-viewed west coast sun that sets regardless of the attention. More for the vision the tourist brochure conjures up of the medieval mariner who appeared on this horizon the other day.

The most famous of the European mariners on his pioneering voyage let down Kochi. Vasco da Gama landed further north on the west coast near Kozhikode in 1498. He did catch up with Kochi soon enough but before that another Portugese landed here.

European couple who run a heritage hotel

Fort Kochi Warf Custom House. A dilapidated building on the waterfront yet to be noticed by the heritage-conscious

The Kochi story begins with the grand arrival of Admiral Cabral in 1500 on Christmas Eve like Father Christmas. To the scribes who followed Santa Claus too, history began here, that very neat moment. Over the next four centuries, they kept coming to create a surfeit of records. Enough for the tourist guide to find high points to keep the visitors enthralled.

To the locals and the coast's travelling traders then, Admiral Cabral's men hardly seemed like makers of history. The sailors from Lisbon, in tatters, looked famished, unwashed, and weather-beaten.

A beggar from Karnataka in Viking headgear, hoping to match the Kochi lore

A far cry from the current arrivals, from the world over, who land in climate-controlled carriers and go about in designer leisurewear. They are on a holiday to an old world European town at Asian costs, and the tourist guide knows what to tell them.

A foreign tourist with a local friend

Now a hotel, this house once belonged to the popular singer Yesudas

Brooke Bond Bungalow, on its way to be made over into a heritage hotel

If you want to get a true gist of this historic sweep, the guide insists, Kochi is the place.

How about Goa which has a longer all-Portuguese history and better beaches?

Kochi got the Dutch and the British too, counters the guide. That's a lot more heritage.

We both have the serial heritage to thank for—the guide's job and my book depend on it.

Senior Soman, autorikshaw driver and raconteur

When did Kochi's heritage come alive? On earlier visits, till the 1980s, I had barely noticed it. Then across the Calvetty Bridge, no longer than a city bus and once no less than a Euro–Asian border, a fine aroma of spices floated into Fort Kochi, from the Mattancherry Bazaar in native Kochi.

Not always strong enough to subdue the odour of the stagnant waterway under the bridge. This cocktail perfumery of spice and slush has since given way to the ubiquitous scent of lemon grass oil, the basic stuff that goes into mosquito-repellent skin creams and body sprays that tourists douse themselves with.

Calvetty Bridge, once a Euro–Asian border

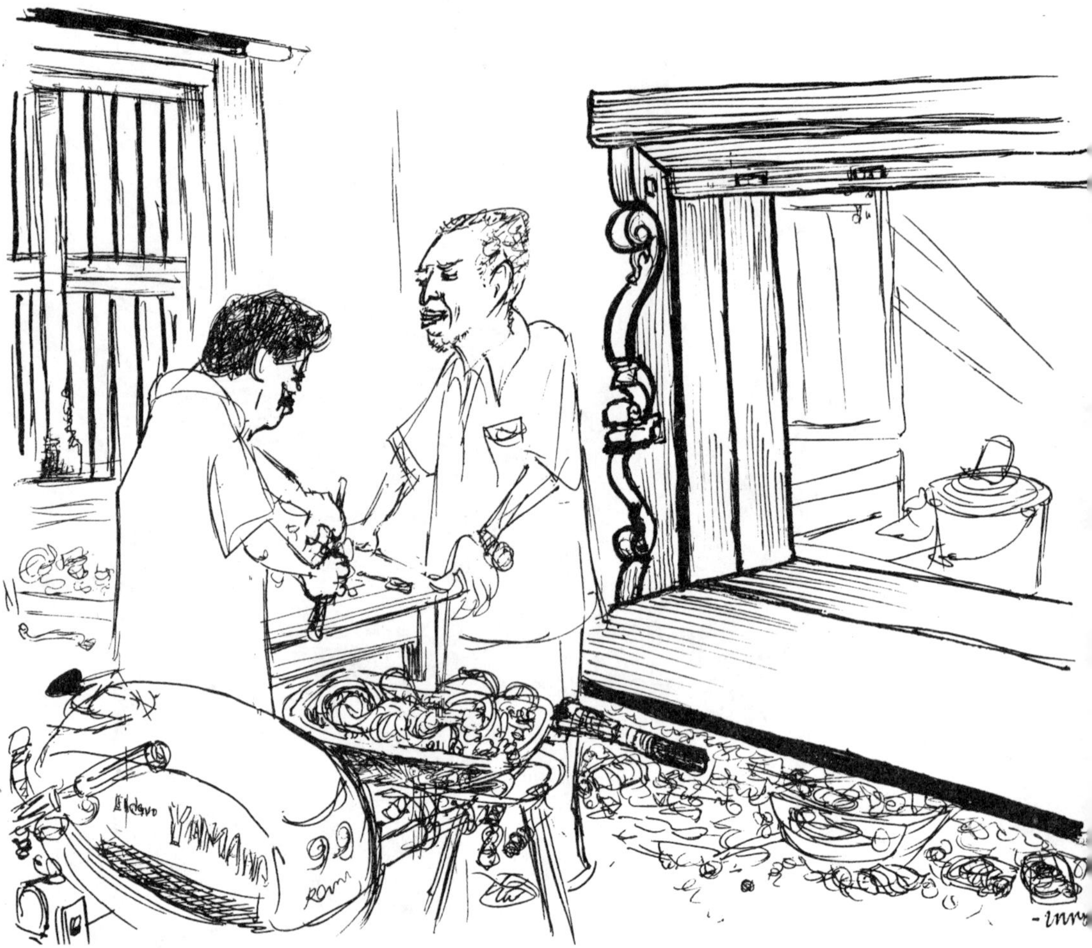

Mechanic Titus working on an outboard boat engine brought by Mohammed from Lakshadweep. The improvised shop floor is part of a typical vintage Kochi house

Even on a sweltering April day, there are evidently touristy clusters moving from one heritage site to another like a bunch of bees, following the rehearsed drone of the guide. The spiel is a string of snatches from the past, a simplistic slideshow.

Since most tourists aren't exactly visiting scholars, they walk around half-listening and clicking pictures of '500-year-old' churches, '300-year-old' Dutch windows, '400-year-old' tombstones and the as yet undated sunset over the Arabian Sea.

Just about everything except the fishermen on little canoes fitted with rusty Yamaha outboard engines, are a couple of centuries old, or so you are assured. Geriatrics would feel embarrassingly young here.

A biking tourist stops to let the temple elephant go by

> In half a muggy day, half a millennium of heritage!

In the evening I find the morning's old-world seekers at the beach shacks unwinding with tender coconut water, Kerala's trademark soft drink. More potent stuff is served elsewhere.

Morning at the beach

Kabir, Nazar and Shemnath at a beachside fish stall

Fresh palm wine in a vintage home-turned-tavern

'You must visit the place,' urges a local acquaintance. 'Not for the potion but to sketch the tavern that works out of a heritage building.' Picture perfect anachronism awaits me. Imbibers empty tall bottles of white palm wine relaxing in a period setting with a family altar.

Family altar in E.A. Manuel's house

From the waterfront to the watering hole, everyone seems high on heritage. Can't get away from the semi-millennial stuff. You can't shake it off during the day and it sneaks up in the dark.

At the river beach. Chinese nets and a rundown building abandoned by a touristy Kathakali centre

As I walk back from the tavern, the sudden evening storm lifts me like the trade winds that powered early sailboats to these shores. Blown back into the safety of the hotel, shaken and drenched, I look out to see the darkening silhouettes of the avenue trees. More than any other sight and sound, these trees mark Fort Kochi.

The rain trees of Fort Kochi →

Every view of the town is prefixed, suffixed or bracketed by these rain trees apparently brought by the Portuguese from Brazil.

Of low timber value, this sleepy plant, as locals call it, was left alone to grow big with leafy serpentine branches and cast its dopey shadow on the town.

Besides, it serves a civic function as a high-rise signpost. If you lose your way and stray out of Fort Kochi, old-timers will tell you to look for the tree top to get your moorings back.

> The tree is a graphic editor too. Its many limbs stretch any which way, to come between the eye and the town's must-see. It dwarfs or foregrounds the much-touted monument, virtually moderating the hype that surrounds it.

Those who want a picture-postcard view of Kochi had better get back to the laptop and digitally alter the photographs they have clicked. My guide didn't tell me so but these trees, I gathered, have a more valid pedigree than much else here.

The tree is a graphic editor

Most manmade structures around are in fact a lot newer than their stated vintage.

'Tea Pot', a new old-look restaurant

Nothing unusual. All heritage spots hawk heritage.

A commercial for a hair shampoo being shot. The period setting is a favourite with ad filmmakers

Ivan Stanslaus D'Costa with his retainer Xavier in his living room – Kochi's vanishing Eurasian setting

This is however, no fairy-tale town with an uncertain antiquity. The Kochi story is dotted with calendar events. Its standard opening, the European advent, happened precisely at the turn of the sixteenth century. By then the Europeans had mastered the art of documenting. The written word had arrived. And thanks to sustained European chronicling, you can count more words here than elsewhere in India.

So much material in black and white on an Asian town would be a welcome oddity to the professional historian. But what's in it for a visitor like me? Long, meticulous accounts that leave little to imagination? One big yawn?

The first hour spent with the first random primer on local history dispels any such fear. The quill, it appears, was wielded as enthusiastically as the sword—for defence, offence and sundry ceremony to generate serial chronicles. Not a dull moment when you look back. More so, because looking back is a work in progress.

Fort Kochi was built as much with parchment and paper as brick and mortar and is still being restored by masons and wordsmiths. With image and text—the very mix that makes a comic strip.

Only, the Kochi comic seems far too animated. History stretches here from one speech balloon to the next and even before it can puncture the first, a third one comes along.

Three major European powers, the Portuguese, Dutch and English, captured Kochi and a fourth, the French, came pretty close to it. The first brought engineers to build a fort and scribes to build up heroes.

The Dutch demolished the fort and built a smaller one but failed to cut down the preceding icons to size. The British who followed soon enough were eager to erase more that was Dutch rather than what was left of the Portuguese. The result is far from a neat sequence of hype and wipe.

*What's often pointed out
as the remains of the Portuguese fort*

Kochi's surviving chronicles tell residual tales that are anything but predictable and hence eminently readable. Barely halfway through the history primer, I find two surprises:

The place has seen a lot more action than you imagined. Its projected heritage has its share of cut and paste jobs.

Much of this vintage town has been razed and redone through many battles and a couple of fire incidents, one bad enough 'to smelt every coin, copper, silver and gold in the Volkart Company's strong room'. Most of what you see has been rebuilt or relocated.

Before it became a Basilica, for long years, the Santa Cruz Cathedral stood on the waterfront. Reduced to a warehouse by the Dutch and shelled down to a flagstaff by the British, it was eventually restored at the present site.

Santa Cruz Basilica. A cathedral since 1558; declared Basilica on 23-08-1984

What about the older St. Francis Church which is the first site I sketched?

It survived but after near-death. The Dutch packed it with gunpowder and it was all but blasted when the soldier in charge of the operation developed last minute qualms. Chronicles credit him for his a pan-Christian vision that cut across the Catholic-Protestant divide. He invoked the name of St. Francis of Assisi, to which the authorities relented. The Dutch had no scores to settle with the pre-Reformation saint, after whom the church was named. So it was spared.

Not all Catholic outfits had such luck at the hands of the Hollander. The Portuguese had built here what has been hailed as Asia's best library then and it became an obvious Dutch target. Priceless parchment and paper stood burning for five full days. The unseen library is part of the tourist lore.

Yet another void stares me in the face ...

Where's the fort in Fort Kochi?

Inside St. Francis Church

There were in fact three of them. The first little fort was built by the Portuguese who went on to rebuild a bigger one. The Dutch levelled and replaced it with a reduced version which in turn fell to a masterly shell fired from an 8-inch mortar by the British forces under Major Petrie's command.

As I was looking around for any vestige of any fort in the vicinity, a local enthusiast pointed out the undersea rubble at the beach that comes into view like a giant turtle shell at low tide. To which of the three historic forts did this debris belong?

Couldn't have been the first which wasn't much of a fort to begin with, just a double lined row of coconut tree trunks held together by mud. Of the other two, Kochi predictably vouches for the older.

Is this how matters of antiquity are settled in these parts? When in doubt, pitch for 'more ancient' heritage? Then the town's signature trees must be the only ones with any organic continuity—birth, growth, reproduction, decay and death. The rest is a suitably ambiguous heritage.

Kochi's signature rain trees

Now, don't assume that the immediate past is any less ambiguous than the distant. Clarity doesn't necessarily improve with time here. In fact the least vaguely stated event in Fort Kochi's life is the earliest, its genesis. There is singular consensus on the port town's origin, perhaps because it is attributed to geography, not history.

From the Western Ghats into the Arabian Sea, forty-four rivers run across Kerala. Of these all but three flow into the sea. When one of them acts up, it has a mere hyphen-long cartographic stretch to vent its spleen. Much fury remains unspent where river meets sea. The effect could be telling as it turned out during an unusually heavy monsoon in 1341.

Periyar River in spate overflowed, desilted and deepened the backwaters off this obscure fishing village and a navigable harbour was born. The birth pangs finished Malabar's mother port, Muziris, which got silted in the process. A major archaeological expedition is on to look for this long-lost harbour, celebrated by historians as an emporium of trade between the East and the West since antiquity.

A glimpse of the Chinese fishing nets through the rain trees

Kochi should be doubly thankful to Periyar. In one sweep, the river gifted a harbour and finished a competitor. Some of Muziri's trade evidently switched to the new port that was waiting to be baptised.

The sailors and traders who spoke Malayalam called it Kochazhi, 'Little Harbour'. The Chinese called it Co-Chin, 'Small China'. More appellations followed from Sanskrit Gosri (prosperous with cows) to Biblical Cocha (a variation of Cohen). In sixteenth and seventeenth centuries, European tongues found amenable variations—Cocym, Cochym, Cochin, Cochi ...

To the Portuguese Kochi became 'Little Lisbon', to the Dutch 'Homely Holland' and to the English 'Mini England'. In his day, the European master must have felt quite at home here. And when that happens, he finds plenty to write home about.

For close to four-centuries-and-a-half in this stamp-sized town, the sword was drawn, the gun powder was dry and the quill was in full flow.

The swordsmen and muskateers are gone.

Chronicles remain.

Vypin waterfront

Little Lisbon

French visitors looking at old Portuguese maps in 'Brunton Boatyard', a heritage hotel

The Portuguese-built St. Francis Church that escaped Dutch ire. Vasco da Gama was buried here in 1524

As I progress from the primer to the next paperback on local history, I begin to wonder how many muses can dance on the head of a needle ...

For a place little, homely, mini and all of one square mile, Fort Kochi has had a steady stream of inspired recording.

It began as a trickle, with the early arrival to the new port of Chinese sailors, Jewish merchants and sundry travellers. Some of whom kept records like the fifteenth century Chinese voyager, Ma Huan, who was part of Admiral Zheng He's treasure fleet.

More than the Chinaman's tales however it is an Italian's one-liner that finds repeated mention in subsequent annals. Niccolò de' Conti, who arrived overland in 1440, came up with this classic quip: 'China is a great place to make money and Kochi to spend it.'

Vypin Water front

Surely, if moneys made elsewhere were being lavished on this town, more money was waiting to be made. Lisbon's shoppers sensed it and they got here in just sixty years after Conti—not a very long time in the then Malabar or Europe for that matter.

As the overseas sailors and traders from Lisbon got busy on these shores, the accompanying chroniclers turned prolific. The written word was there to stay and the Portuguese celebrated it by setting up a library here—considered the best then in Asia. Eventually, their manuscripts turned out to be only as unyielding as their garrison. Both fell to the Dutch.

The Hollanders were compulsive chroniclers themselves, so much so that as early as 1748 their governor in Kochi, Julius Valentyn Stein van Gollenesse, concluded that history had ended. Much reading, he proclaimed, was a weariness of the flesh and more than enough had been written on Malabar. This hardly deterred the Brits from adding their own tales.

Views of the town

Chronicling continued and is still on. Every single day brings tourists who stand and stare at this heritage town. Most of them seem content to merely float in the great vague sense of an immense past. And while at it, shoot anything in view with camera, camcorder and the multi-tasking cell phone. This in turn creates an everyday digital chronicling—one that lends itself readily to alteration.

The good old scribes, low-tech, made up with literary devices to ornate their stories. They were quick to grab Kochi's big miss, the Gama voyage, as a prologue to their account. It is a familiar flashback that sets the stage for Cabral's grand arrival. In 1498, Vasco da Gama landed in Kozhikode, Malabar's key port town, post Muziris. The second best west-coast ports were Kollam to the south and Kannur to the north. Kochi Harbour (b.1341) was then a mere century-and-half old.

Despite Conti's rating it had to wait for the footfall of a big-ticket history maker. Mercifully not for long, thanks more to politics than commerce. Politically, the early European chroniclers found nothing familiar in the tapering southern Indian peninsula then. The huge land mass didn't seem remotely like a Euro-grade empire or kingdom.

The region consisted of vassals and near-vassals or at best, as in Vijayanagara, an uneasy network of chieftains flexi-loyal to an overlord. The local turf-sensitive potentates, all the while at each other's throat, made what little history they could.

Even the best of the lot on the west coast, the ruler of Kozhikode, had no overseas concerns that matched his grand title Samudri (Lord of the Seas). He merely sought to lord it over the neighbours, mainly the Raja of Kochi. He did run a well-oiled trade town with systems and protocols in place, a fact widely acknowledged by chroniclers but not in the least by the coast's most illustrious visitor, Vasco da Gama.

After ten months of valiant sailing, the voyager seemed to have found no comfort on land. Chronicles are replete with accounts of his violent mood swings—as though a certain arbitrariness and brazenness would add to his glory. Had the man been a lot less prone to extreme acts of cruelty he would have looked as laughable as a comic strip hero like Hagar the Horrible or Captain Haddock minus his pipe and innocence.

Scribes credit Gama with a missionary zeal that hardly redeems his image. He is projected as a superior Christian out to elevate the natives who he mistook for heathen Christians.

Vasco House behind St. Francis Church.
Vasco da Gama is believed to have stayed here

He had his task cut out: upgrade his lesser brethren to full scale Christianity; drive out the Muslims, Kozhikode's trusted allies and take over their trade. Gama hardly took a couple of months to thoroughly antagonise his first host.

Chronicles are silent on why the great argonaut set sail to an alien land without doing any homework. Before he discovered the all-sea route to Malabar, the destination was already part of the European trade circuit. Portugal wasn't venturing on a blind date with India.

An elderly woman in the typical Kerala Christian homewear

Well before Gama set off, a fellow-Portuguese, Pêro da Covilhã, had been commissioned to do an overland reconnaissance of Indian spice trade and sniff out a possible sea route to Malabar from Europe.

He had kept a journal of his travels through Kannur, Kozhikode and Goa and couriered it to Lisbon through a Jewish shoemaker and voyager, José de Lamego. If at all Gama bothered to browse through it, he certainly didn't apply the knowledge in these parts. He seemed as remarkably ill-informed as he was ill-tempered.

After its historic Asian connect, Lisbon badly needed to make friends in its colony and that task fell upon Admiral Pedro Álvares Cabral who headed the second Portuguese expedition. He too first reached Kozhikode which was by now fairly wary of the Portuguese. Cabral's opening moves on this coast town read like a Gama postscript. He did nothing remotely balmy and after unleashing enough fury on his first port of call, sailed off to Kochi, to earn a hearty welcome there.

As the enemy's enemy, Kochi emerged as a natural European ally. Born at the cost of Muziris, Kochi was beginning to grow at the cost of Kozhikode.

By now, having settled down to document Kochi at some length, the scribes turned to matters native. Kochi King's ceremonial reception to Cabral is described vividly. The King himself is shown as a much modest man though, with a lot less wealth and even less pomp than the Samudri, the first contact high of the Portuguese scribes on this coast.

Far too accommodating, the King had allowed his traditional trade partners, the local Muslims as well as those from the Middle East, to reside in houses with stone walls, a privilege in those days, close to his modest palace, 'itself by no means an imposing edifice, and badly furnished.'

Interestingly, all Kochi rulers come to be credited with this unerring modesty barring a particularly high-handed one who lived up to his sobriquet, Sakthan Thampuran (The Mighty Lord).

Like all modest men who typically don't close their options, the king who hosted Cabral extended extra courtesy to the Europeans. He allowed the Portuguese Factor and his men to sleep right in the palace compound.

From a Chinese fishing net, Vypin Church across the river

'Dutch Palace', built for Kochi's king by the Portuguese and later repaired by the Dutch

Cabral's anger seems to have been spent in Kozhikode. One finds a much redeemed man in Kochi, almost phlegmatic, even tactful, by Gama standards.

Cabral seemed to have had something like a perspective too, for he didn't let down his host at the first opportunity. He politely turned down offers of cheaper pepper and other spices from the rulers of Kollam and Kannur. His only tactless act was his departure without saying as much as a bye your leave to the King, carrying with him the Nair hostages who were sent on board as sureties, and leaving behind his factor and men to fend for themselves. The Rajah kept his cool and took good care of the Europeans till the next fleet arrived. Diplomacy of sorts was beginning to happen between Europe and Asia.

In three years flat, the Portuguese were permitted to build a fort and they named it after their King Manuel, the Fortunate. Not much of a fort, just a glorified fence made up of trunks of coconut trees stacked together with mud.

Looking back, all one can say about the imperial structure is that it was bio-degradable. The concern obviously wasn't ecology. The limited construction was in deference to the Rajah's reservation against a stone or brick structure for any building other than a temple.

The fear of God soon gave way to more earthly fears, as the Portuguese presence increased and with it the hostility to Kozhikode and the threat from its firepower. An extended fort was eventually built with sturdier stuff.

Meanwhile, even before Cabral returned to Lisbon, a third expedition, under a nobleman João da Nova, was on its way to India. King Manuel was a man in a hurry. For good reason. Gama had returned with merchandise valued sixty times the cost of the uncertain expedition. And Cabral was soon to return with equally considerable cargo ranging from 'spices and drugs, too numerous to detail, to diamonds, pearls and rubies including a very colourful one that weighed seven carats and a half.'

Portugal on an overdrive privatised its monopoly sea route to India. In 1500, orders were issued permitting merchants to undertake expeditions for a fee: a quarter of the value of the cargoes brought back.

A popular old mosque in Kochangadi

The historic Holy Cross where the historic Coonan Cross Oath was taken in 1653

The sea route, however, did not become anything like the latter day Suez. The offer had no takers. Without the backing of an imperial state the risk was far too much. Risk is too mild a word. The voyage itself often depleted half the crew and the rest found little peace on land. Nor did they seek any.

Every move the Portuguese made on the Malabar Coast was action-packed. The very concept of conflict resolution changed with the European advent. The local potentates' familiar tiffs over territory became sideshows to the full-scale battles the Portuguese waged with the Muslims.

Trade itself happened like commercial breaks in a televised war movie. Muscle and money chased each other all over the place. As the most welcoming port to the Europeans, Kochi got squarely caught between the two. The survivors of every succeeding Portuguese fleet returned from here with spicier tales to tell their grandchildren. Of these the spiciest is the war of 1504.

Kochi for the first time saw a proper WAR— a warfare vastly different from the stylised skirmishes of local chieftains that commenced at daybreak on an auspicious hour and ended at sunset.

The scribes' job was made easy by the presence of an eminently inflatable war hero. They are unstoppable in Duarte Pacheco's defence of Kochi against the forces of Kozhikode, the might of its Muslim ally and the intrigues of petty powers through several battles that in all lasted five long months.

Copious blood and ink were shed in Kochi. Casualties ran to tens of thousands and truth could well have been the first. The Portuguese superman's post-war glory however, hardly lasted. Back home, Pacheco was imprisoned on charges, later proved false, and was formally rehabilitated and left to die a pauper.

A fate the vanquished Samudri could have readily attributed to heavenly retribution. The Kozhikode court was packed with formidable soothsayers and Brahmins whose curse could stop a marching army—the local archers and wrestlers perhaps, surely not the Portuguese.

Aboobacker, cinema operator, praying at his mother's grave at Calvetty Mosque

Calvetty Mosque

Believed to be the house where St. Francis Xavier stayed. The doorway carries a marking attributed to the Dutch East India Company (VOC)

The Europeans themselves were not vastly rational. They had their own share of superstitions such as shying away from any vital task on Fridays.

One Portuguese governor who skirted this norm was Afonso de Albuquerque, though faith-led in other ways.

The Kochi scribe was happy to get a superstar like him close on the heels of an action hero like Pacheco. A true doer who went on to do enough on these shores to ultimately earn the epitaph: 'And let him that does more than this take precedence of him.' You can't afford to be predictably Friday-phobic if you have to sail, trade, negotiate, mediate, maim, kill, compete, plunder and loot, all in the interest of that mighty enterprise called empire building in an alien land.

Albuquerque expanded Gama's scrappy success story into a novel. Certainly an autobiographical novel and there are no prizes for guessing who the hero was. The man had a self-image that was supremely heroic.

Albuquerque's role model was apparently Alexander the Great, whose biography in Persian he had read. He found time to actually read in the midst of a million tasks? Believable because either the soldier/sailor himself had a way with words or at least the sense to spot the right scribes who ghost-wrote for him. Archives are full of his long, persuasive letters to the Portuguese king that justified his expansionist moves here.

The elaborate prose comes as a foil to the quick-paced annals of an action-packed era.

The Alexander clone's triumphs are liberally listed. He fought as fiercely as the legendary Greek, let the local rulers rule once they were humbled and match-made on a grand scale, like him. He was the first to persuade Portuguese soldiers to marry native women by offering generous rewards. In one stroke in Goa, he conducted 450 weddings after duly converting the brides to Christianity. To the newlyweds, he allotted houses, cattle and land.

Albuquerque knew that land grabbing was as vital as seafaring to the consolidation of the first European power on the Indian soil. He captured Goa twice and built it into a city with many castles and a mint, held a fortress in Kozhikode and rebuilt Kannur's mud fort with stone and mortar. And to Fort Kochi he gave a fort that was finally fort enough. A large pucca fort that enclosed most of the town. He also deployed seven large elephants at Kochi's shipyard on the beach.

Strangely, Kochi doesn't acknowledge so colossal an achiever even half as heartily as it does Gama, by no means a popular figure in these politically correct times. Gama to his credit died here on Christmas Eve, exactly twenty-four years after Cabral arrived.

His tombstone is eagerly pointed out to every tourist who steps into St. Francis Church. Albuquerque's sole memorial is a weather-beaten signboard near the Aspinwall House. Hardly the tribute to an imperial hero his countrymen referred to as 'The Great'. Almost everyone except his illustrious predecessor in Kochi.

Vasco da Gama's tombstones. 'Here lay buried Vasco da Gama who died on Christmas Eve of the year AD 1524 at Cochin until his remains were removed to Portugal fourteen years later'

Bishop's House established on 04-02-1557

The lone voice of dissent hasn't gone unrecorded because it came from Portugal's first Indian Viceroy, no less. Dom Francisco de Almeida clung to his viceregal post refusing to hand over power to 'a fool and a mad man'. He was content with sea power and thought Albuquerque was overreaching himself on land. The new man, the Viceroy thought, was building far too many fortresses with far too few men to run them in the absurd hope of mounting an instant empire. Dom Almeida was convinced he had already scaled the peak and wasn't ready for a bigger climber who had showed up all too soon.

Nothing more is heard of Almeida; Albuquerque takes over the annals.

> A fortuitous factor that cemented Euro–Asian ties in those fluid times was the longevity of the rajahs of Kochi. In the entire sixteenth century there were only four successions to Kochi's throne. If you made friends with Portugal, you even lived longer.

Yet why is Kochi today indifferent to its most celebrated visitor from Lisbon?

Having captured Goa, Albuquerque was partial to it much to the resentment of his own countrymen in Kochi.

Lourenço Moreno, the Factor of Kochi, and Antonio Real, the Chief Alcaide, saw in the rise of Goa the loss of Kochi's primacy and they went to the extent of complaining to the king of Portugal. The protest went unheeded.

As its eastern enterprise was growing into something like a government, the Crown must have factored in a proportionate rise in intrigue. Lisbon would have received much mail airing conflicting interests and the king must have kept a large waste bin.

In any case by the time the snail mail reached Lisbon, Albuquerque would have made a few more decisive steps towards Goa. When he eventually shifted the capital from Kochi to Goa it must have been a lesser concern to Portugal's king than to Kochi's officials then and its tourist operators today.

Kochi doesn't seem to have missed a central government that was perhaps getting too close for comfort. In any case, at the best of times the Portuguese managed to create no more than a porous system that leaked copiously.

A factor that compounded the problem was strangely the Portuguese urge to record, which extended to commerce as well.

Next to the sword they wielded the quill and the eraser (if there was one then) with equal enthusiasm. Complex rules were drafted only to be flouted, frequently modified or altogether rolled back.

If you want to know the bureaucratic maze that was in vogue then, you only have to look at the trade agreement of 1585. Under an elaborate arrangement, different customs duty rates were fixed for different categories: resident Portuguese, non-resident Portuguese, unmarried Portuguese men, Christians resident north of Cochin and a sundry lot that included Christians resident south of Cochin, local Christians, Muslims, Jews, Venetians and Armenians.

You can divide and rule. You might even subdivide and rule. How can you sub-subdivide and hope to rule?

A phenomenal customs house was envisaged at the port where all goods were to be sorted from a single table. Sadly there is no record of how this single window system worked, if at all it did.

All we are told is that the over-regulated Kochi was a happy place. A visitor to Kochi in the 1580s, Gasparo Balbi, rates the place as 'after Goa the first city that the Portuguese have in India, and of great commerce in drugs and other goods.'

Much perverse help came from the local European administration. It licensed pepper movement and looked the other way. Shippers carried cargoes many times bulkier than the prescribed quotas.

The result was that while pepper and opium remained on paper contraband items for a good part of the sixteenth century, both were being openly traded, most certainly with the connivance of both the states at work.

As if one government wasn't enough, Kochi had a native parallel regime that levied lower tariffs. Traders, Portuguese included, made full use of it at the cost of the Crown by diverting their products through the local princely channel. Diarchy was even better for making the extra buck.

Among the few legacies from this era, the flair to sidestep the system remains in Kochi's chromosomes. It manifests in many forms from outright lawbreaking to inventive conning. This town is a favourite setting for Kerala's filmmakers to tell stories of toughies who extort, romance, kill, die or redeem.

Locals freely talk about an underbelly which to be precise is under water. There are extraordinary divers here who can yank out overnight many things, from a berthed ship including its anchor, and use the seabed itself to hide the booty. Less-than-licit income is socially accepted, so much so that in some circles while fixing a marriage, due consideration is given to the groom's extra income from the 'side' (meaning smuggling/gray market).

The period setting is a favourite with ad filmmakers

There is a new breed of money makers who target the hard-currency tourists. They endear themselves to the visitors and follow up the contact through emails requesting aid for ailing non-existent mothers and infirm fathers long dead.

E-mailer seeking overseas charity at an Internet café

Palm reader Raju, foretelling the future of visiting Londoners

Sob stories quite often click as they did way back in the 1600s.

In 1610, an anonymous chronicler recorded, 'Today there are no rich men in India, save in Kochi.' Strangely, soon enough the town's Portuguese residents rose in chorus to send out SOS messages. A colossal doom, it would appear, had suddenly descended on the place. Dom Diogo Coutinho, Captain of Portuguese Kochi between 1614 and 1627 wrote to the kings of Portugal and Spain that the town was depopulated, its commerce was finished and there wasn't enough revenue to pay even the ecclesiastical expenses.

Other scribes suggest that things were nowhere as bad. As a prosperous trade town excessive demands were being made on Kochi to finance Portuguese expansion, next only to Goa which had turned into a capital of coercion. A way out was to sound suitably poor.

Kochi's Portuguese elite made a fine art of broadcasting poverty. An official's account from those days describes the plight of respectable women who had taken to begging by the day or prostitution by the night. He says citizens have turned to God for help and goes on to give a graphic account of the forty-day-long penance they undertook. By nightfall, people set out in processions, some in sackcloth and ashes, some flogging themselves, some crawling.

There must surely have been some in the town eminently capable of such theatrical exertions. Kochi's very own theatre that came up as a Portuguese hybrid. 'Chavittunatakam', is nothing if not a feat of physical endurance. Based on Biblical, mythological and historical themes, a single play could last up to a fortnight. Actors, well drilled in Kerala's martial art 'Kalari', had to voice musical lines loud and clear in those mike-less days, dance for hours on end and perform Olympics-grade gymnastics.

In its heydays this stylised costume drama had stunning live action that involved the actual hanging of a performer—scaffold, rope and all. As the hangman got into action, the hero marched in on horseback with choreographic precision to draw the sword, slash the rope and rescue the victim. If the hero was tipsier than usual or the horse distempered, you would have a dead man on your hands, in glittering costume. Mercifully no such mishaps have been reported.

This heritage theatre is being revived in a safer, milder form today. Naturally, because now you can only draw upon part-time enthusiasts who undergo the training but are not hard enough to undertake deadly acts on stage. And they go about on low-powered motorbikes, not on horseback.

When the slightly built, forty something Britto Vincent parks his bike and walks in, I know who he is because I have been briefed by Nelson Fernandes, the living compendium of Kochi's culture. As the mild-mannered Britto begins to chat, his voice and gestures betray a rigour that rules out any further doubt.

Nelson Fernandes, writer and longtime activist in Kochi's cultural life

Britto Vincent, an actor in Chavittunatakam

You can still find in Kochi disapproving old-timers who hark back to the grand old days of this theatre. Like these purists of traditional art, many annalists of the Portuguese era have their own good-old high point—which is clearly the Albuquerque phase.

Post Albuquerque their enthusiasm diminishes barring a spurt here and a blip there.

The chronicling curve dips almost mirroring the decline of Lisbon's power over India. There isn't much more to be found in the records on the lapsed Portuguese capital except the return of Gama in 1524 to die here.

> The Portuguese who sought to lord over the three Cs—Commerce, Conquest and Conversion—didn't quite measure up to the image they sought to project. They did a great deal of commerce that leaked all over the place. Their idea of conquest ranged from seasonal coastal presence to agoraphobic fortress building.

Conversions that came with a reward in the early Euro–Asian marriages were soon overshadowed by zealotry at its worst in the Goa inquisition. Worse still, their bungling on all three counts was recorded by the friendliest of historians who might have exaggerated their deeds and misdeeds to a fault. The faults show.

Like our voluble TV journalist, the hyping annalist must have inadvertently blurted out a lot of truth. In the process, making the military conflict look more sensational than it was, the era more eventful than it was and the hero even more absurdly heroic than he was.

Even before Lisbon's men were packed off, a keener bunch of record keepers were approaching Kochi. The Dutch, with the English close on their heels, were already sniffing around in the Indian waters.

The Jews who successively fled serial repression all the way from Europe and Middle East were already among the prominent subjects of the Kochi King. The equally enterprising Konkanis, the Portuguese drove out of Goa, too had found relative comfort here. Neither had reasons to like the Portuguese and their opportunity to speak out was close. On the other hand, the town's considerable citizenry of Portuguese descent dreaded the newcomer. When the Dutch finally took over in 1663, friendly and hostile eyes witnessed their deeds.

Now don't assume that Kochi's chronicles suddenly turn polyphonic enough to yield an even-handed picture. No such boring prospect.

The plot, if anything, only thickens.

A music concert in progress at Vasco Square

Homely Holland

Dutch Cemetery

A World War II fire extinguisher that found its way from the port into a local antique shop

While the Portuguese Admiral Cabral came to Kochi chiming on Christmas Eve like Santa Claus, the Dutch marched in, all guns blazing.

The first thing the Dutch gave Kochi was a long war that involved more intrigue than action. Not the stuff that pleases the scribes. Nothing remotely as heroic and well-scripted as Duarto Pacheco's defence of the town under the Portuguese. Much wheeling and dealing had to happen with neighbouring chieftains, the local Jews and the native state's prime minister, Paliath Achan before the Hollanders could call Kochi their own. The town fell only after two-year-long engagements that included a pitched battle with the queen at the local palace.

For the first time you spot a woman who made it to Kochi history but not much more. The scribes who later get voluble about Dutch and Jewish women have little use for an Asian woman, a loser to boot.

Choir quartet practicing at St. Francis Church

Were the Dutch poor readers who learnt little from the follies of the much-chronicled Portuguese era?

Once they took over, they unleashed the very same religious frenzy that doomed their predecessors on these shores. A good century–and-a-half later in 1663, when Europe was beginning to change!

It was 21 years since Catholic Europe's best-known victim, Galileo, had died a prisoner in his house. Protestant Europe had learned to live with a bright 21-year-old Cambridge science graduate, Isaac Newton.

More than this newfound openness, it was the Thirty Years' War (1618–1648) between brother Christians back home that got played out here. Where else can you show that vestige of vigour except in your colony?

The new Protestant power in Kochi was out to erase every Roman Catholic sign, symbol and structure the predecessor had left behind. They destroyed, by an account, ten out of the twelve Catholic churches inside the fort. Catholic priests were banished and the laity told to convert to the new faith or live without religion, die and burn in hell, a foretaste of which was currently on offer. Some fled, some complied if only formally.

The Dutch zeal to baptise and christen extended to the inanimate as well.

> After the customary plundering of the town, the streets were renamed. When they built a new fort here, the Dutch named every bastion after a province of the Netherlands: Gelderland, Hollandia, Zeelandia, Utrecht, Friesland, Groningen. For a change, they showed a little levity by calling the small canal they dug to ply laden boats from the harbour to the fort, Overissel, after the grand waterway in Holland.

After such cleansing of faith the Hollanders congregated at the St. Francis Church. More cost-conscious than the Portuguese, they took over an existing church rather than build a new one.

Mason M.B. Jacob in CSI St.Francis Church Cemetery

A bigger eyesore to the Dutch, the Santa Cruz Cathedral was spared because it had better uses. Then situated close to the harbour, it became a convenient warehouse for 'sugar from Bativia and cinnamon from Ceylon; as well as nutmegs, cloves, iron, copper, cordage, rice, pepper and other articles.'

Morning walkers outside Santa Cruz Basilica

Pleasantries done, the Dutch got down to business. Literally. Right through their troubled stay in Kochi, the scribe cites cold commerce as their main concern. They did flex their muscles across the trading table but only when their business interests were at stake. They were dragged into local conflicts because there were far too many disputes to start with among the one too many powers eyeing the region.

Kochi with its proven commercial worth had become strategic to every one of these players—the rajahs of Travancore, the sultans of Mysore and the Samudri of Kozhikode, not to mention the most strategising of them all, the English. Each one of them the Dutch befriended and antagonised at some point or the other. Even the embedded chronicler couldn't have made much of so shifty a hero.

The Dutch are known in this coast not for the battles they won but for the one they lost. In Kolachal, in 1741, to Maharajah Marthanda Varma of Travancore. Chroniclers almost gleefully refer to the commander Captain Eustachius de Lannoy, who surrendered, promptly switched sides and served Travancore honourably ever after. After tasting blood in the Portuguese era, the scribes were obviously getting miffed with the new European forays that hardly threw up big events or a war hero like Pacheco. The Dutch battles, perhaps equally well fought and no less bloody, could have merely gone underreported.

Wayside sermon in Calvetty at daybreak

The Hollanders didn't get a particularly good press on these shores. Unlike the Portuguese whose major critics were Muslim chroniclers, from the outset Dutch moves were being watched by fellow Europeans as well. Neither their Portuguese predecessors, who wouldn't exit in a hurry, nor the English who already had a foot in the door could have been empathetic appraisers.

How do you get the Dutch side of the story? Shouldn't be difficult given the massive material they piled up. But the mass of routine everyday recording fed moths and ants more than the historian. The 19th century chronicler, Francis Day, British Kochi's Civil Surgeon, rummaged through Dutch government records numbering many hundred volumes. 'Some effaced by time and more mutilated by insects.'

'VOC', the abbreviation of Vereenigde Oostindische Compagnie (Dutch East India Company), is a marking of high heritage value

The officials from Holland were obsessive record keepers. The Dutch East India Company (VOC) which ran Kochi must have spent half a day at work and the rest recording work.

The governor kept a diary and handed over to his successor a detailed memorial of his tenure, often voluminous. Governor Moens' manuscript ran into 553 pages. Besides, meticulous account was kept of all mail received and dispatched. And any letter from a neighbouring king was translated and filed away, duly classified.

Such elaborate paper work to administer a square mile of Fort Kochi?

The Dutch were reporting to a power structure back home that makes the inverted pyramid look like a toy. The top-heavy outfit that ran the empire was in Bativia, not in Amsterdam, and it consisted of the governor general and a council of nine 'high nobilities' and under these the commandeurs and councils of the several provinces.

Not an enviable situation if you had to operate in the then Malabar. Asian powers had turned smart enough to play one European nation against the other as the Samudri did with the Dutch and the English. The Hollanders were waiting for prior approvals in triplicate before they made their next move on quicksand.

The Dutch were golfing in a soccer field. Incidentally, it is the golfing Brits who found some merit in the Dutch system. The English East India Company eventually put in place a similar reporting structure and one would have expected their annalists to probe the prototype a bit more. How did the British work a system that did the Hollander in? Perhaps the situation was saved by new technologies—steamships and the telegraph that came and busted distance.

Sea bathers at the beach

Meanwhile, all we are told is that the Dutch governors in Kochi lasted on an average a good five years, which incidentally was as long as it sometimes took for a treaty signed locally to get ratified by Bativia and Amsterdam. By then events invariably overtook the pact.

A yacht seized by the authorities for straying in, since auctioned

A Kochi house redone as a heritage resort

The men from Holland come across as slow moving objects in a racy polity, altogether unworthy of the imperial task that came their way. Even when they quickly reversed their initial proselytising zeal and won back natural traders like the Syrian Christians and Jews, they only got reluctant credit. For want of war and politics, chroniclers gleefully turn to matters less public—the everyday life of the Dutch men and women in Kochi. A domestic lifestyle that could have only been sustained by a considerable retinue of retainers, read slaves. Slave trade was one Portuguese legacy the Dutch inherited without qualms.

Dutch governor, Van Gollensse's handing over report in 1743 mentions '37 male slaves and the 16 girls who are still in the depot here.' One item in the Malabar Coast accounts reads, 'By taxes on slaves exported from this coast f. 81-0-0. i.e. Rs.48.' There were local gangs that kidnapped children and sold them to the French at Mahe and the Dutch at Kochi. Despite pleadings from the English, the Dutch refused to abolish the practice. When the English moved in, nearly every domestic in town was reportedly a slave.

More than the plight of the slaves what seems to have driven the scribes is the sheer opulence of the master. What follows is the kind of voyeuristic prose we still see in the media, sought to be justified by a suitably moral tone of disapproval.

The Dutch housewife, often neglected by husband and children, spent most of her time managing her female slaves. Chewing betel nuts and leaves all day, she did minimal housekeeping.

> The drawing room was ship shape, the rest of the house a mess. The house itself had walls at least ten-feet high and two-feet thick and the heavily pillared gateway was quite narrow. No two walls were parallel and no two windows or doors alike. Before marriage however the lady had a charmed existence. All she cared for was her personal appearance. She had a wardrobe that matched a prima donna's and hairdressing skills which were no less.

The men too get their due place in the chronicles. The master of the house rose at six, smoked his huge pipe till seven and sat down to a sumptuous breakfast. After this he went back to his pipe refilled by the slave in attendance. More slaves then got to work to slip him into elaborate costume. Suitably attired, he received clients and attended to his business for an hour or two. By then he had worked up an appetite for a lunch that makes the breakfast look snacky—boiled or grilled fish, salt or fresh meat, and a profusion of vegetables, with oil and butter sauces, washed down by copious spirits of Holland or other spirits. After a further drag at his pipe, he napped. At three, over a cup of tea or coffee, he began a long gossip session with visitors. By nine, he was ready to polish a meal by no means lighter than lunch, after which he retired with his pipe, the day's deeds done.

Kochi's Hollander looks like the cartoonist's ultimate challenge. How do you roll the bear eating Obelix, the pipe smoking Popeye and the punch drunk Wizard of Id into a single comic persona? If you ate like a pig, smoked like a chimney and drank like a fish, how did you survive at all? A question best left to the medical historian.

Cochin Club

The scribe's verbal caricature of the Hollander extends from home to workplace. Over-indulgent at the dining table, the Dutchman is shown over-regulating at the trading table.

He held on to a pricing system as though it was holy writ. Having fixed a minimum profit margin of a 100 per cent in every transaction for monopoly of pepper in exchange of military aid, he sat back in the hope that business would proceed on autopilot. The times were too choppy to let any such thing happen.

The English, French and Danes must have run rings around this frozen arrangement and while at it combined much pleasure with business. The Hollanders, to be fair, entertained in great style. It was during the Dutch rule that Kochi got its pub lore. Thanks to an enterprising innkeeper who paid the authorities to acquire sole rights to host visitors here. The hotelier after expenses including pay-offs, accumulated Rs.50,000, a neat sum then.

Conti's one-liner about this town being a great place to spend seems truer a good three centuries later.

The laid-back Hollander vis-à-vis the daring, dashing Portuguese is the refrain of the typical Kochi chronicler. And whenever the sedate Dutch chose to act, they didn't win many laurels either.

Who'll cheer you for burning down a library?

The Dutch made matters worse by building a smaller fort—an act that is seen as a pat symbol of their limited vision. All one can say is that the reduced fort, variously described as a half to one-third to one-fifth of the original, hurt Fort Kochi's pride proportionately. Finally, a Hollander did something to frustrate the fault-finders and redeem his lot.

> Hendrik Adriaan van Rheede tot Draakestein, the Dutch governor between 1673 and 1677, commissioned a grand treatise on Malabar's flora. Running into twelve volumes of nearly 500 pages each with 794 copper plate engravings, *Hortus Malabaricus* (The Garden of Malabar) was eventually published in Latin from Amsterdam between 1678 and 1703. It has descriptions of 742 plants sketched with striking accuracy by a Carmelite Father Mathaeus. Apart from botanical features, the medicinal properties of the plants are detailed.

There weren't any differentiated botanists in the then Malabar. The best minds on plant life were those who practiced herbal medicine. The governor roped in a prominent Ayurvedic physician, Itty Achuthan, and three Gowda Saraswat Brahmin scholars Ranga Bhat, Vinayank Bhat and Appu Bhat for this momentous work.

The Dutch made up for their poor history with brilliant botany. Almost. Recent research by Dr Savitri Preetha has taken away a little sheen from this prodigious Dutch project.

She has unearthed a pre-Van Rheede compendium of the flora of southern India commissioned by an English factor at Masulipatnam on the east coast. She notes that the order of plants illustrated with paintings in this collection of some 120 folios bears a striking resemblance to the arrangement of the *Hortus Malabaricus* that succeeded it beginning with the coconut palm and followed by the other palms and useful trees.

Thank God the early chroniclers didn't chance upon this work. They would have rubbed in the fact that van Rheede wasn't such a stand-alone achiever.

In any case Botany didn't help beyond a point. Only to the extent of reducing the harangue. Nitpicking continued. Long-time Dutch friends like the Jews and Konkanis did nothing much to buck the chronicling trend. The Jews were busy penning their own tales and the Konkanis in Kochi never seem to have sat down to write anything beyond their account books.

One reason the Dutch left such a poor impression here could well be linguistic. The scribes who came during the Dutch and British days sourced Kochi primarily through Portuguese, which was the first language they learned here. The link language must surely have coloured their perception.

Lisbon's best insurance turned out to be its language. The Dutch got constantly compared and contrasted with its predecessor by scribes who sourced in a rival language.

There is an unmistakable moral/religious ring to these accounts too. Recurring digs at the inferior quality of Dutch faith. Hollanders get blamed on several counts of disloyalty—to nation, woman, language and liturgy.

Look at the extended blame list: as late as 1888, a good 225 years after the Portuguese left, their local descendents gathered in Vypin Church to mourn the death

All that remains of the gateway to the Dutch Commandeur's ortha (botanical garden). Now a housing colony with over a hundred houses

of Dom Luis I, king of Portugal. The vicar sang a solemn dirge and the local newspaper commended him for his musical effort. The Dutch descendents on the other hand retained no such sentiment towards Holland. They equalled their predecessors only in vice. An unmarried tobacconist, sighted in Dutch Kochi, kept a virtual harem of a dozen women. Again, the Dutch language vanished soon after the Hollanders exited. In just a matter of three decades, there were a mere 24 in Kochi who spoke Dutch. Portuguese continues to be spoken in Goa and till recently in Kochi.

Further, Latin liturgy was more robust than most things Dutch. The Roman Catholic Diocese survived through the Dutch phase and even retrieved many souls lost. A good many Dutch converts reverted to Catholicism no sooner than their masters left. With equal ease, the military men who stayed on, mostly mercenaries, switched sides overnight to serve the new master. The English forces returned the compliment through matrimony. Quite a few officers married into Kochi's Dutch families. From the Dutch flock, employable men joined the new civil administration and sailors sailed under the Union Jack. One prominent citizen came up with a remarkable way to adapt. He just dropped the Dutch 'van' from his name.

St. Peter & Paul's Church, founded on 08-05-1881, being spruced up for the 450 year celebration of Kochi's Latin Catholic Diocese

A neo-vintage restaurant in Elphinstone Road –
'228 year old Addys, since 1776

If there were remarkable scribes who stayed loyal to the Hollander, we don't see them. The last target of this era's scribe is the Dutch pension roll. One that generated eminently readable trivia. The English continued to honour it in the hope that VOC would compensate. But the income from the settlement of Rs. 75, 000 wasn't enough to pay even the POWs. The new regime had on its hands a dole list that included a retired hangman on a monthly pension of Rs. 5, an invalid sergeant on Rs. 8 and another soldier on Rs. 24 who complained that he was getting less than a drummer boy.

Preceded by a language that outlasted theirs and succeeded by a power a lot smarter, Kochi's Hollander looks like the neglected middle child.

But then there is no last word on Kochi's past. Santa Claus' next Christmas gift could well be a Dutch-friendly scribe or two.

Mini England

Not a tourist, the rare resident

The pulpit in the Santa Cruz Basilica, perhaps one of the few things that date back to the Portuguese era

The English began their reign here with a classic misnomer. They razed in 1803 the last of Kochi's forts, the one the Dutch built, and called the fort-less town 'Fort Cochin'.

After creating one void, they followed it up with another. They shelled the Santa Cruz Cathedral down to a flagstaff. For nearly a century this early Portuguese place of worship on the waterfront remained only in public memory. It was finally restored at its present site.

When I went there to sketch, a church official pointed out the only thing in the nave that dates back to the Portuguese era—a pulpit that was saved because it travelled to the Vypin Church and back.

French visitors looking at old maps

The British did a bit of renaming too. In the case of Princess Street, no less than gender change. To the Hollander it was Prince Straat.

Princess Street, Prince Straat to the Dutch

And who else but the Englishman could have come up with a name like Loafers' Corner?

Loafers' Corner

The English sense of humour, however, took its time to surface in Kochi. Their first three decades here was a long indifferent pause. And when they made their first major move, it was enough to wipe out every smile. The most anglophile of chroniclers can't find a better euphemism than a 'foolish act of vandalism' to describe the fury unleashed on the town and the calculated indifference that followed. Even the resilient Jew was with his back to the wall. If there was one left standing.

This, from the Brits! One thought they'd be more image conscious than their predecessors! Not here.They took their time to warm up to Fort Kochi, develop stakes here.When they took over they had more mundane things to attend to like the Dutch pension list. Image management wasn't a priority. The treasury itself didn't look very good but that didn't prevent a couple of early English commanders from prospering. Worse, they were too brazen to evade detection. Summoned to London, they were tried, fined and imprisoned. Barring these misdemeanours, in the early English decades there was nothing much to report.

For a good 30 years Kochi remained much as the Hollanders had left it.

A 1925 chapel in Meccenzie Lane

In retrospect, this turned out to be a painfully long and eerie wait before the firing squad marched in. The long-lulled town was unprepared for the sudden assault. Hierarchical to a fault, Kochi's officers were merely waiting for orders from superiors in London. When the orders finally came in 1806, they accomplished in cold blood what the much-maligned Dutch did 143 years back. They blew up the fort and the much-admired buildings that housed the Dutch East India Company (VOC).

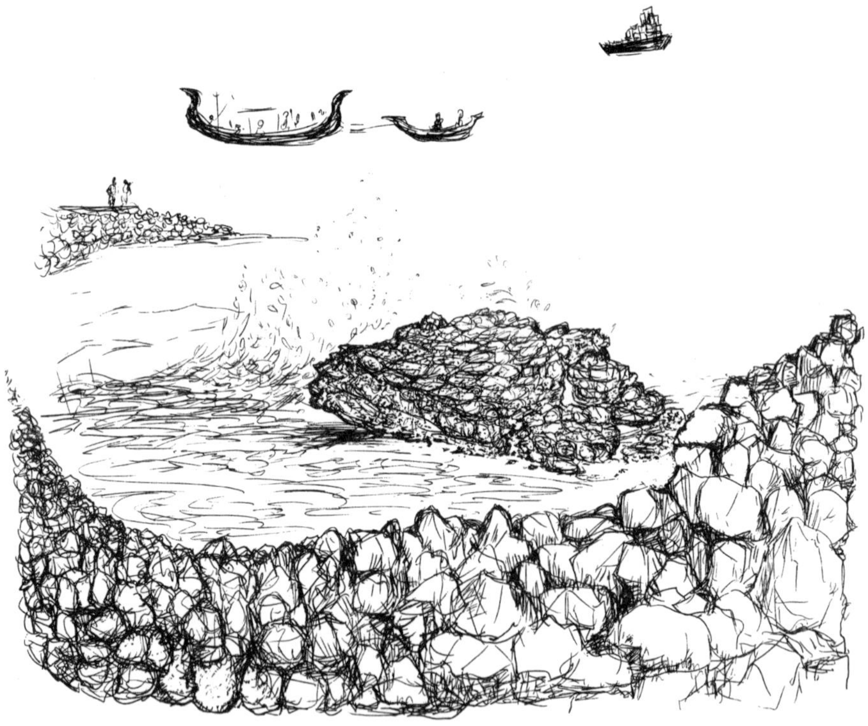

What's often pointed out as the remains of the Portuguese Fort

Even private buildings were so badly hit that they had to be buttressed. A feature today's visitor takes as integral to Fort Kochi's architecture. When new buildings are erected in these touristy times, buttresses are added for good measure as a concession to heritage!

A restored, newly buttressed corner house

If there was anything worse than the demolishing spree, it was what followed. Kochi was left to die a slow death. For two long years the debris was left uncleared, the drains choked and the roads blocked by rubble. An eyewitness account goes, 'the place had taken on a look of ruin and desolation that deepened the general depression. The people languished. There were no schools. No public buildings.'

The Kochi heritage look, overdone with buttresses

St.Francis Church Lower Primary School, Estd. 1817

It took an epidemic to wake up the authorities. When it finally decided to sit up and govern, the East India Company had a raging rebellion on its hands, and none it could call a friend.

All it had was a formal ally—the Rajah of Kochi. Though glad to get rid of the Dutch, the king developed no instant chemistry with the English. Unlike his ancestor who had received the first European power to these shores more like an equal, he found no comfort with the new methodical meddlers. Much had changed since the Christmas Eve of 1500 when Cabral came with the twin offer to trade and finance the Rajah's feud with his Kozhikode overlord.

In 300 years the native king, as much as his traditional foe, was a reduced ritual presence. Irked by the patronising British, Kochi Rajah's utmost act of defiance was to receive in diplomatic silence a loaded message from the Dutch prisoners of war (POWs) that came in the form of a gift—a portrait of Napoleon.

The hint couldn't have been broader. The British forces in Kochi were anticipating a French assault and His Highness if he so desired had an option: to shed one European yoke for another. The POWs were actually Francophile Dutchmen on parole whom the British had pensioned off.

Althara Bhagawati Temple

The king went no further. The closest reported French contact of the royalty was a hairdresser, Jacques Valois from Pondicherry, who made wigs to amuse the Rajah. And he apparently didn't get paid for his efforts. The best the king could do perhaps was to watch his rebellious prime minister in concealed glee and of course in diplomatic detachment.

Prime Minister Paliath Achan, who had lately developed a mind of his own, led a few assaults into the British town with a Travancore Nair militia in tow. With predictable result.

It wasn't easy to awe the Englishmen. The British were already a tropicalised lot when they stepped into Kochi. They had been hovering around for quite a while. In fact, they had begun to look eastwards a good 100 years before the East India Company was formed.

John Cabot, an English merchant of Venice, and Vasco da Gama had set off to shrink the world the same year, 1497. Cabot didn't make it because he went north and west and ran into hurdles worse than the rough seas Gama faced as he headed south and east.

A mosque in Calvetty working out of a declared heritage building

In the service boat to Fort Kochi from the mainland

It was almost a tossup between the English and the Portuguese. Wonder what if the Merchant of Venice had made it to Malabar instead of Lisbon's Lear? Kochi could have been the Raj's capital instead of Kolkata. Never mind, the Brits would have shifted the capital sooner than Albuquerque.

The English made the preceding colonisers look like amateurs. They were thoroughly prepared when they set out to explore. King Henry VIII, not in the best of terms with Spain and the Pope, couldn't support maritime adventures as well as his Portuguese counterpart, Dom Manuel. Also, he chose to send his men out in better warships and these took a while to build. He wouldn't settle for fort-like floats where deckhands doubled as soldiers and fought like pub brawlers. Henry VIII created the Royal Navy and equipped it with cannons that fired a deadly broadside from the portholes, often rated in chronicles as a clear leap in ocean warfare.

Though the Portuguese snatched the maritime medal in round one, the British were preparing for a whole tournament. Only when they were rehearsed and ready did Queen Elizabeth sign the charter for the Hon'ble Company in 1600. In another 100 years when the Brits were eyeing Kochi, their navy became superior to all rivals: the French, Dutch and Portuguese. They were virtually unbeatable when they came with a detailed project report that was drawn up for sub-continental scales.

The grand scale turned out to be the problem here. Kochi was a mere speck in the British radar. The British arrival was bad news to the Kochi chronicler. From war correspondent and global market watcher, he was relegated to the municipal beat. Once the Portuguese India's capital and then the seat of Dutch governors, Fort Kochi was reduced by the British to a municipal town.

Less than a district headquarter. The town became the sub-division of Malabar district run from, of all places, Kozhikode. This was a blow. Central to Kochi's legacy was its running feud with that unmentionable northern native state. And the brazen Brits with a stroke of the pen re-established Kozhikode's overlordship. Five minutes' walk from the once viceregal Vasco House, a mere sub-collector presided over Fort Kochi from the beachside Bastion Bungalow. From where, if it is of any consolation, the Crown's representative got a stark view of the sun when it finally set on the Empire in 1947.

Kochi had long been a vantage point to look at the Portuguese and the Dutch. A fair share of European history, two centuries of it, played out in this tiny Asian town. The good old chronicler was witness to many colonial games on show here. Right in his front yard, history was home-delivered.

Views of the town, bracketed by the town's trademark rain trees

In the British scheme of things however, Kochi was no more than a port town. It is only after many years and much lobbying by local merchants and port authorities that the harbour's potential was fully appreciated. In fact, in their early years the Company considered the town eminently dispensable. It wasn't sure whether to stay on in the first place.

Only after the Anglo-Dutch treaty of 1814, did the Brits decide to keep Kochi as barter for the island of Banca which they ceded to the Dutch.

Deprived of big-time players, the chronicler turns to the sundry Dutchmen left behind, a lot that mirrors the scribe's own diminished status, which ironically does in no way restrain his glee.

Pay reduced and perks from private trading gone, the Dutch pensioner is pictured as a petulant litigant. As one who ran around raising claims over his entitlements.

The last Dutch governor, Van Spall, himself carried on a protracted dispute over his private estate, biding time for a Napoleonic win that he hoped would reverse his fortunes. He was in time deported to Bombay but his heirs kept the claim alive long after Bonaparte became history.

This bungalow belonged to J. Thomas & Co. a familiar trading house of Kochi

Bastion Bungalow, where British Kochi's highest official stayed

Lesser souls buried their valuables. When the surgeon of the British hospital dug up his garden, he chanced upon a cache of three lakh musket flints. His landlady promptly advanced a claim.

Like any place with a history of uneasy successions, Kochi too has its legacy of buried treasures, some dating back to the last days of the Portuguese. Before exiting, some of them found a macabre way to vault their wealth. They buried alive their African slaves along with their valuables.

Called Kappiri Muthappans (Negroid Elders), these dutiful ghosts are supposed to guard the booty till the true claimant arrives. Enterprising locals periodically wine and dine these spirits in the hope that they would get sozzled enough to lower their guard.

A good 400 years after the Portuguese left, when a house on Rose Street was pulled down, two walled-in skeletons were found, and while demolishing an old house near the Dutch Cemetery, the contractor came across a chained skeleton.

In either case no treasure was declared but the contractor soon built a well-appointed bungalow for himself.

Now that the one-square-mile land itself is a touristy treasure, who'll bother to dig it up? If you did, you may not find any treasure. But many believe you'll come across a wide spread of subterranean architecture.

> A whole network of tunnels. There was apparently one from the Bishop's house to the beach, another from the British Residency again to the harbour, and under the yard of the Pierce Leslie Company was a hub of four tunnels one of which led to a bunker, roomy enough to house the British residents during the 1857 revolt.

In Kochi today, the tourist operator seems more excited about tunnels than the archaeologist.

> In the wee hours of 29 December, 1808, Colonel Colin Macaulay, the first British Resident, is believed to have escaped through one such tunnel. He had as guide, his loyal clerk, De Mello, who knew his way about in the town's underground passages. The existence of tunnels is the simplest explanation for the survival of the Colonel under siege by a marauding flock of six hundred (by some accounts a thousand) armed rebels led by Paliath Achan.

The sensational escape seems to be the high point in the Resident's stint. He doesn't get much credit for what he did before and after, in these parts.

David Hall, long in disuse, since restored as a café gallery

The most loyal chronicler couldn't have overlooked his role in the town's mindless destruction in 1806. The Resident did contribute some silver lamps to the synagogue in Jew Town, if that helps. And the fact that he was the uncle of Lord Macaulay who came to be celebrated in British India's annals is mentioned in passing as redeeming trivia.

After the Resident's recall in 1811, the British Court of Directors offers an excuse for the man's 'want of a conciliatory temper'. His disposition may have been affected by his imprisonment in Srirangapatanam under Tipu Sultan!

Sounds familiar. He only did unto Kochi's natives what Mysore's natives had done unto him. We saw how the British pillaging of Dutch Kochi was explained, as nemesis catching up with the Dutch for what they did earlier to Portuguese Kochi. In the eyes of the colonial chronicler how come nemesis stops abruptly at the immediate predecessor?

Aboobacker, cinema operator, praying at his mother's grave at Calvetty Mosque

A hotel in Calvetty in memory of the late Mysore Sultan who nearly got here. He seems to be a bigger favourite than Vasco da Gama or Albuquerque

Santa Cruz Basilica School

After Macaulay, Munroe and Cullen were two residents who did enough to get a decent obit. Munroe opened schools and is rated a tough administrator. He himself wielded the cat-o-nine-tails on recalcitrant and corrupt officials. Both, known to be good revenue collectors, had twin charge that included the neighbouring southern state of Travancore as well, where Cullen however, threw his weight about.

The lieutenant general launched a war of nerves against King Swathi Thirunal, who was anything but a hate object. An egalitarian ruler and a legendary composer, the Maharajah remains a fond presence wherever Karnatak music is sung. The British cold warrior instead has to contend with an obscure memorial in a corner of Kochi, a traveller's inn named after him. Mercifully no more worthies are mentioned who lent their names to wayside stopovers.

'Western' Willie, the chef at 'Teapot'

Amidst the humdrum officials who followed, the odd striking non-official comes to the news-hungry chronicler's rescue. Rev. Samuel Ridsdale was one. By the middle of 1826 this priest from the Christian Mission Society (CMS) arrived from Kottayam to an indifferent Kochi. The dingy, cheerless house he managed to rent was in his own words unfit for an Englishman to live in. The spirited missionary decided to build a house for himself and a school on the ruins of the Dutch fort. There was some confusion here over the building sanction he had sought from the British authorities in Madras (Chennai). A soldier who was assigned to discuss the matter and possibly stop him from poaching public land was literally brought down to his knees with a volley of homilies.

Quite likely because Malabar had had some singularly persuasive priests. The German missionary Samuel Hebich with an impressive vocabulary of 522 English words had converted almost every officer of the 36th Madras Native Infantry. More articulate and with an ability to preach in the vernacular as well, Rev. Ridsdale was to eclipse the German pastor with a sole star conversion.

By then he had built his house. The imposing structure with palatial columns and arches was however frowned upon by brother missionaries. The priest insisted he spent his own money which wasn't much because he had recycled the masonry of the demolished fort.

The Church of Our Lady of Hope (Nossa Senhorade Esperanica) in Vypin

A 1922 wayside chapel

True to form he kept the house for himself, didn't pass it on to his parent mission. After his death, his widow decided to sell it. For one who taught the three Rs at her husband's school, Mrs Ridsdale's 'Rithmetic was poor. She left out a zero when she wrote down the price, 50 pounds instead of 500. The good lady stuck to the deal.

Ridsdale's evangelical zeal matched his grand taste. He targeted no less than a prince from the Kochi royal family. When a boy was born to the Rajah in 1813, the palace astrologers predicted a great scholastic future for him. The best of tutors were engaged for his traditional schooling in Sanskrit and for more he was sent to Fort Kochi—to learn English under Ridsdale. The pastor's school had as students, Christian converts, Jews and untouchables. The Reverend Father, aware of the caste taboos, took it upon himself to privately tutor the prince and his constant companion, Anand, a Gowda Sasraswat Brahman. Quick on the uptake, the pupils lapped up the Testaments, old and new.

You can't teach much English without bringing in the Bible. In this case, the effect went beyond the academic. Soon the prince and his friend were ready for the formalities. On a hot April day of 1835, the young men were led into St. Francis Church and through the baptismal motions. A considerable congregation stood breathless to welcome the prize catch. This was where St. Francis Xavier himself preached shoeless, hatless and in torn cassock—and saved the souls of faceless fishermen.

At long last the face had arrived. Little wonder that one recent chronicler goes thoroughly overboard. He looks back across centuries and does an eyewitness account interleaving the weather outside and the proceedings inside.

The filmy report goes like this: As the solemn ceremony wears on, a dark cloud appears in the April sky and a pre-monsoon storm builds up. Lightning. Thunder. The swing fans of the church sway like the sails of a ship in a hurricane. Just as the two upper caste Hindus shed their sacred threads and kneel to rise as newborn, a deafening thunder bolt strikes. Unfazed, the choir sustains the refrain *Jubilate Deo.* Before the ink dried on the baptismal register, the skies cleared but did not fall.

That evening, led by Anand's father and the prince's elder brother, a hostile crowd collected outside Ridsdale's house where the town's European gentry had gathered in full strength to toast the priest. The British were in full command. There was nothing much the mob could do except entertain itself with some rituals. The angry brother performed the last rites of his lost sibling at the Parade Ground after which everybody went home.

Anand, christened John, became secretary to a Syrian Bishop. Constantine Rama Varma went to Madras (Chennai) and joined the Grammar School there. The blue-blooded suffix 'Varma', wasn't shed. It surely had its demonstration value. Five years later the royal convert set off for Antioch but on his way fell ill in Mumbai and returned to Kannur. Here he joined the Basel Mission, married a school teacher and settled down. In 1856 he was ordained Rev. Jacob Varma. Next year while attending to small pox patients he fell to the virus.

With Kochi's history unravelling steadily into such sensational current affairs, it was about time the everyday chronicler stepped in. It took a while longer for the town to have its own professional journalists though. And when that happened, it did with a bang.

In 1860, Kochi got its very own print baron. William Brunton, the founder of the engineering firm Brunton & Co. raised Rs.3000 to start the first newspaper here, *Cochin Argus*. The weekender seems to have had a combative editor, Francis Rice, who spared none. Soon two rivals appeared, *Cochin Chronicle* and *West-Coast Spectator*. The authorities, often targets of Editor Rice, encouraged the two to merge. The double barrelled *Malabar Mail* however remained a poor second to the *Argus*. The next thing you find is the much-feared fighter-editor of *Argus* in a new docile avatar, as the chief secretary to the Rajah of Kochi. If you can't lick them, hire.

A closer competition to *Argus* came from a new weekly, *Western Star*, started in 1864 and edited by Henry Walker who also ran a printing press by the same name. Almost in tow, he launched a Malayalam paper *Paschima Tharaka*, the title a literal translation of Western Star. Before long a Gujarati merchant, Devji Bhimji, invested in another language paper *Kerala Mithram*. Its claim to eventual fame is that it was edited by Kandathil Varghese Mappila who went on to found *Malayala Manorama*, India's biggest language newspaper today.

Local Gujaratis warming up for the day

Over a Century old, the Gujarati temple for Samudri Devi, the Goddess of the Seas

Whatever happened to the 19th century print boom? No sign of it on Rose Street. Fort Kochi's Fleet Street didn't stay so for long. The *Argus* trundled along for half-a-century, the rest had shorter runs. Kochi's flashes of enterprise went with a herd instinct, a combo-trait still very much evident. If the newspaper was the next thing to do, everybody from shop-floor owners to sundry merchants started one. Spice trade looked good, so everyone including the officials traded. English was the language of power, so anyone who mattered sent the kids to learn the language. Including an unsuspecting king.

Sanoj Rahman, bike tourism promoter

The latest in this series of self-limiting trend cycles however, looks a bit overwhelming. The entire town is now in the grip of an entrepreneurial monoculture, tourism.

Almost every house and shop on every street, including the Rose Street, and all bungalows on the river and sea fronts are ready for visitors who arrive round the year. It will take increasing ingenuity to spread them across the seasons and rotate them when the season peaks. You can't build much more horizontally or vertically. Backwater-bound, sea-bound and heritage-bound, the tiny tourist delight has a problem that isn't difficult to guess—space.

Rose Street, once Kochi's Fleet Street

Babu and Varghese, fishermen leaning on one of the four anchors of 'Lord Willingdon', the dredger Sir Robert Bristow brought from Scotland in 1938 to deepen the harbor. It dredged along till it sank in 1979

Early last century, a unique visitor came along who not only made no demand on space but actually created floor space in these parts. Tourism was far from his mind. Sir Robert Bristow was an engineer who came to dredge a three-mile-long channel and deepen the harbour into a modern deep-sea port. In the process he heaped hectares of reclaimed land into an island. Which was eventually named after his patron, Lord Willingdon, the governor of Madras and later India's viceroy. In his early days here, a lady asked Bristow why he must disturb the restful charm of the backwaters by building a busy port. He told her bluntly that he didn't think British Kochi was exactly a thing of beauty or a joy forever. The engineer knew his Keats.

Through the 20 years he was here Kochi did grow on Bristow.

He came here in 1920, soon after the First World War, and foresaw the outbreak of the second. He knew Kochi must be not just a mercantile but a naval port. His was an unenviable task. His project needed the concurrence of four governments, two railway companies, naval authorities in Bombay and competing merchant communities.

In an early incarnation of the technocrat, Bristow combined endless committee work with hands-on engineering. To be precise, legs-on. To study the wave action during the monsoon, he stood still in waist-deep sea water and ended up with sore skin on both legs. After all this if the poor man didn't become a nervous wreck, it is not because he was exceptional but typical. He exemplified the best of the Brits who had by then professionalised the art of running a colony. They had method. They toiled through the day but their evenings and weekends were their own. They had their clubs and outings.

This new class then was the first in these parts to strike, what we now call the right work-life balance. They didn't exactly sit and sulk even through the grim global slump, which Kochi's Chamber of Commerce cites in 1931–32, as a good enough reason to go slow on their pet harbour project itself. In their very next annual session the very same chamber, British-run, grants a five-year loan to the Cochin Club of Rs.5000 which they quickly enhance to Rs.6000 repayable with five per cent interest over 15 years. If this isn't work-life priorities, what is?

Early morning outside the Laurel Club which comes alive only by sundown

Bristow had the leisure to appreciate 'the simple life but wholesome lives of fishermen on a Malabar Sunday morning, shielding themselves from the rain and mending their nets.' After a hard day's work and a game of golf at the nine-hole course in the Residency at Bolghaty, he stands and stares at the 'last level rays of the sun sifting through a bamboo grove.' The little caddie boy interrupts his reverie and the quaint conversation that ensued is recorded in his memoirs, *Cochin Saga*.

Pretty, Master; pretty.

Who telling you pretty?

No Master telling. I seeing pretty. Master also seeing?

Bristow was his own chronicler and perhaps the last big European Kochi watcher. A virtually unchallenged one, for there are no competing chronicles, though some remarkable Indian raconteurs like Justice M.S. Menon worked with him.

The Raj began to write back much later.

Attendant Devassy at United Club

Karl Marx, Other Jews and the Like

Football fans at a night tournament in Parade Ground

Parade Ground

When the Union Jack was finally lowered at Parade Ground in 1947, Fort Kochi was freer than the rest of India. In one go, 444 years of uninterrupted European dominance ended here. (You get this neat figure when you count from 1503 when the first fort was built). The one-square-mile Euro-zone instantly became part of an Asian wonder, an against-the-odds democracy then. Across the border at Calvetty Bridge, native Kochi didn't hold back at all. It was the first princely state to join new India, even as its southern neighbour, Travancore, went in kicking and screaming.

Before long the Kochi merchant's worst fear came true. In his presidential address to the Chamber of Commerce in 1948, J.S. Bruce summed up his post-war worries—rising prices, labour disputes and demand for higher wages, all of which opened up fresh fields for communist activities. He wasn't wrong. In 1957, the newly formed province of Kerala, Kochi included, elected a Communist government. The chamber session that preceded Bruce by ten years had recognised trade unions on the express condition that they wouldn't encourage class war.

No street wars were fought here in 1940s and 50s. The Brits didn't have to hunt around for underground tunnels to flee. Seasoned colonisers, they negotiated a smooth exit. A peaceable Gandhi helped.

This was true of the whole country. Fort Kochi was special. It had seen a lot more of colonial rule and misrule. And when that ended it wasn't Gandhians who were readying to take over but followers of Karl Marx, no advocate of gentle power shifts.

Kochi's communists were however busy waging trade-union battles. In any case, how could they have mounted a showpiece anti-imperial revolution on a one-square-mile municipal town? The town itself had changed hands far too many times to tell tragedy from farce. What stayed through a succession of masters was a flow of commerce that brought in its wake a range of ethnic groups and languages. And a unique culture of co-existence.

If Kochi needed lessons in survival, it didn't have to look far. More than the revolutionary Jew, it was the local Jew who had a demonstration effect. Even before Marco Polo.

A memorial for T.M. Mohammed, the much loved Communist leader of Kochi, at Kunnumpuram junction

Synagogue in Jew Town

Jews were sighted on the Malabar Coast as early as 1167. Ever since, they had been through occasional glory, some peace and much turmoil. One zone of great Jewish comfort was Dutch Kochi, which vanished all too soon. When the British virtually finished the town, an eyewitness was almost ready to write off even this Judaic phoenix. Thoroughly drained by the succession war between his Dutch friends and the new British power, the Jew had barely found his feet when the deferred disaster struck.

He must have stayed on because he had enough religious conviction to hope. Also because the Jewish settlement had stakes in Kochi. Stakes that far exceeded its numbers—even the most generous estimate of 16000 by Rev. Claudius Buchanan, an avid collector of old Jewish records and manuscripts. The census undertaken by the dewan of Kochi, Venkata Rao, in 1857 however, threw up far less impressive numbers—no more than 1790 Jews in the whole of Kochi state, of which 353 in Ernakulam mainland, 65 in Chennamangalam, 25 miles inland and a mere 419 in Jew Town next to Fort Kochi, their largest settlement. The Black Jews, the ones who intermarried with locals, constituted the rest and they were mostly in Fort Kochi, happy to be away from the White Jews of Jew Town, Mattancherry.

Even within the outwardly cohesive Jewish community there was a black and white divide. Nothing unique to Kochi, they had such subgroups elsewhere on the coast like the historic community of Jews called the Bene Israel (Sons of Israel) in the Konkan region. Kochi's latter-day Jewish immigrants who considered themselves genetically pure and white refused to bond with the earlier settlers with mixed genes. There is a similar divide in the way the divide itself is seen by the chroniclers of the 19th and the 21st century. The former go into elaborate physiognomic description to underline the fuller Jewish look of the new Jew as against the vanishing Jewishness of the older settler, his shapely Roman nose cited as the sole saving grace.

When it comes to women, the gaze turns patently voyeuristic—'scanty skirt, of rich cloth, satin, open from the throat, nearly as far down as the waist.' The chronicler bemoans that once married the Jewess covers her head, no longer cares for her personal appearance, rapidly loses her good looks, and at 30 may be considered quite passé. The contemporary chronicler treads more gingerly and explains the Jewish divide as a cloning of the fractured Malabar society. Like picking up a new language, the Jews apparently mimicked the social milieu they had walked into.

Synagogue in Jew Town, waking up

Synagogue in Jew Town ready to receive the day's first set of tourists

To be functional here the Jews thought it best to be a caste, and to be a caste you had to have sub-castes. A survival formula the Portuguese perfected in the 15th century. In fact, they were the ones who introduced the root word of caste, *casta* meaning lineage, to describe the many-tiered society they found in Malabar. They created a social ladder that was one up on the local one.

Ladder would be a euphemism; the hierarchy was more like a spiral stairway, much coiled. The pure white born in Portugal, their offspring born here, the ones who intermarried with locals, the natives, the local Christians who lived north of Kochi, those who lived south of Kochi, they took all administrative and commercial decisions keeping in view these myriad categories to often produce bizarre outcomes, as we saw earlier when they inked in a trilateral-trade pact in 1585.

Khalid, autorikshaw driver

But the Jews weren't a colonial class that could apportion privileges across such a broad spectrum and at the best of times there weren't enough of them around. True, but given these limitations, they did quite well. They made a fine cocktail of their own Judaic and the host-Hindu mores to perpetuate a complex and durable hierarchical order. White Jews, Black Jews, Brown Jews, those with certified ancestry (a dual one at that), those without, those who could sing hymns in the Mattancherry Synagogue, those who could only sit in the anteroom and pray silently, women who could wear gold in Jew Town and those who had to hop across to the European Fort Kochi to dress up.

Traders in Mattancherry

Lineage, real or invented, and skin tone, selectively attributed to genes or the tropical weather were considerations that overlapped most perniciously, to create social stress that lasted a good 400 years—through the Portuguese, Dutch and British years, through acts of defiance and challenge from within the community—from formidable reformers like A.B. Salem, known in these parts as the Jewish Gandhi.

Reformers have come and gone but the Portuguese *casta* is very much in place in Kerala in diluted and, as your homeopath would tell you, potentised form. If anything, it is the Jewish caste system that might finally disappear, if it hasn't already. Not due to any sudden egalitarian afterthought. For sheer want of numbers to sustain the divisions.

Only about 30 Jews are left and counting down, I hear.

The Jews left the way they arrived, in waves. Some moved to Mumbai and Kolkata after the Portuguese virtually razed down the Jew Town in 1662, quite a few to the homeland soon after Israel was formed in 1948 and many subsequently.

The footbridge across Rose Street that was once part of the building that housed the Koders, the town's most prominent Jewish family

The last Jewish bastion, so to say, in Fort Kochi, was the Koder House, now a hotel. Here a prominent merchant family lived from 1808 till recently in splendid engagement with Kochi's social and civic life. If Kochi's citizenry wanted to see the stereotyped Jew, usurious and insular, it would have had to look elsewhere.

Fort Kochi's old-timers tell me Koders brought them light. The family started the first electricity distribution company here and ran it with a feudal benevolence. When the subscriber was too broke to pay the monthly bill, the payment was kindly deferred. Today the government-run power board will just cut off supply.

Inside Koder House

Fort Kochi Town Square

After the sale of the Koder House, there is nothing much Jewish left in Fort Kochi. But you only have to step out of the unseen fort to find the Synagogue and the Jew Street—the last vestiges of a community that meant a lot to these parts.

The Jews were as good as their Dutch friends in keeping records which they archived with ritual rigour. No document with the God's name on it was to be junked and the Jew never wrote one without invoking the Lord. For the New Jews, recorded evidence was absolutely central to their identity.

As recent immigrants, they had trade contacts as well as knowledge of foreign languages including Portuguese—skills that endeared them to the Rajah of Kochi as well as to his Portuguese friends here. The last, ironically, had reasons to thank their anti-Semitic masters back home. Lisbon drives out this resourceful lot which soon surfaces in Malabar to serve its very evictor's colonial interest!

Destitute, penniless and in the midst of well-entrenched co-religionists, the new contingent had little choice. They strategised right—first aimed for status and waited for money to follow.

Right from the outset they steadily worked towards a virtual aristocracy. Like the new rich who have to look richer, the new aristocracy had to look doubly aristocratic, vis-à-vis the early Jewish settlers. They had no bones to pick with the host community.

The New Jews' claim to Jewish superiority rested solely on written records. They swore by a copper plate, a charter of entitlements from Kochi's King that granted privileges and even a principality to great ancestor Joseph Rabban. This was meant to prove beyond doubt that the New Jew's local ancestry went back all the way to the oldest Jewish settlement in the neighbouring Kodungallur. Besides, they had impressive documents to support their true Jerusalem lineage as well.

This magical alloy of copper and paper, truth and apocrypha, was enough to send the early settlers scrambling for matching evidence. They had to document or perish. In the first two decades of the 16th century, thanks to the Gama connect, Egypt had begun to receive regular mail from Kochi. The mail bag contained endless requests for copies of Jewish texts. Then there was no way the Old Jews could have googled across continents and centuries and found anything worthwhile.

Synagogue in Jew Town and its first set of tourists

Synagogue in Jew Town bustling with tourists

As their hopes rose and fell with the departure and arrival of the mail boats, their smarter kinsmen were steadily inching towards royal patronage. The Rajah of Kochi virtually ruled in favour of the rising lot. He gave them a plot to build a synagogue right next to his palace. (Some chroniclers say the palace came up after the synagogue.) Either way, proximity to power couldn't have been better demonstrated, and that proved the final arbiter.

All was well for the New Jew till the Portuguese went wild. In 1662, the Portuguese on the run, in a scorching spree, burnt down the Jew Town and with it went heaps of parchment and paper. Under the friendly Dutch who followed, he quickly recovered and sat down to write his history all over again. With the benefit of hindsight the effort must have been an amply driven rewrite. The Old Jew was edited down to a footnote. The better chronicler ultimately won.

The late Samuel Hallegua, the widely respected Jewish elder was a ready reckoner of Kochi Jew's history

Kochi's Jew never sought to colonise or evangelise. All he wanted was to belong, perhaps much more eagerly than he needed to. Armed to the teeth, the Portuguese, Dutch and British tried in vain to hold on to Kochi. The Jew managed with a disarming smile. Alice's cat is all but gone, the smile stays.

By the 17th century, Kochi's annalists had already got to see their second European power in action and by the 19th century, the third. Their favourite sub-theme is the relative merit of the succeeding European rulers. Ranking and rating had become second nature to them. Yet they leave the Jews pretty much alone. Like the Jew Street with its neat rows of houses ending at the synagogue, the Jew's much retold story has an opening that only leads to them. No alleys or by-lanes that lead elsewhere. A singular survival saga of a peerless lot!

A bit odd, because you only have to step out of the Jewish quarter and before you reach the parking lot you will find the Kamat Hotel. As much as Koder to Kochi, Kamat is a familiar surname like Kini, Pai, Shenoy and Mallaya—all Konkanis. A community that the chronicler, if he chose to, could race with the Jews.

Come to think of it, there are obvious similarities.

Jew Street. A resident with the morning paper unmindful of the brisk shopping outside his doorstep

The Konkanis like most Kochi Jews fled Portuguese persecution to arrive here. They have a well-preserved identity many centuries old; as Hindus, a caste hierarchy that was a neater fit into the host culture and commercial and language skills comparable to the Jews, not to mention a distinct cuisine, finger-licking good.

Kochi chroniclers have jumped at lesser parallels. Yet they narrate their favourite Konkani story without bothering to note that it resonates with the familiar predicament of the wandering Jews. On their periodic exodus, the Jews always carried the *Torah* (the scroll that states the Mosaic Law) which is central to their congregational selfhood. In the case of the Konkanis it is their idol that travelled.

Sreedevi S. Prabhu, a Konkani elder, at the Sree Gopalakrishna Swamy Temple, a Marathi shrine

Sree Brahma Kshetram, a temple in Amaravati

The Rajah of Kochi had permitted Konkanis to build a temple.

One fine morning in 1719, the idol vanished from the Thirumala Devaswom Temple. It was soon spotted near the beach and was taken to the Dutch governor's house.

The clueless official gave the carved stone to his children to play with. Soon the first lady fell ill and a native doctor traced the cause to the iconic presence in the house. He took it away and kept it for seven years during which time his family members frequently ill fell.

Chronicles offer no clue as to why the good doctor, who brilliantly diagnosed the governor's wife's sickness, suffered in silence for seven long years in the company of the idol.

Rita, a fish seller

The Cochin Thirumala Devaswom Temple in Mattancherry run by the Konkanis

Eventually, the idol was identified and restored to the temple where it stayed put for some 80 years. In 1791, trouble started again when Kochi had an unusually harsh ruler, Rama Varma, better known, for good reasons, as Sakthan Thampuran (The Mighty Lord). He asked the temple to contribute loads of sugarcane jaggery for a royal feast. The trustees refused. The king singled out one of them, Devaresa Kini, and sent soldiers to behead him and raid the Konkani bazaar for good measure. The temple priests panicked and rushed the idol to the Dutch fort for safe keeping. From there it was sneaked out of the state's borders to the neighbouring Travancore. Its ruler was keen to build a temple in Alleppey to house the idol but the priests quietly decided to restore it to its original shrine. Hidden in a food basket, it was smuggled out in a boat bound for Kochi.

Since the idol was thought to bring good tidings to the host state and its absence misery, the Travancore king went so far as to order troops into Kochi and seize it. Kochi sued for peace and palmed off a gold-adorned replica of the idol. The best efforts of Kochi's fine goldsmiths couldn't conceal the fraud. Yet another fake was sent and the once-bitten Travancore men saw through that too. The dispute raged till 1859 when the British government in Madras ruled in favour of Kochi, where the idol finally found peace.

Ginger House restaurant-cum-antique shop

Neo-antiques in Princess Street

If European chroniclers go on about this colourful Konkani story as though it is a comic aside to the serious business of conquest and commerce, the reason is obvious. They find a stone idol less worthy of reverence than the textual scroll of the Jews. Less obviously, it is the textual *Torah*, not a sculpture however sacred that celebrates the written word, in which all scribes develop stakes.

As for idolatry or the aversion to it, a lot has since changed. I see European visitors stepping out of Santa Cruz Cathedral, hopping across Loafers' Corner into Princess Street and heading straight for the antique shops. What could be more pagan than the pantheon of neo-icons ready to be packed and fedexed?

Bicycle stand in a spruced up heritage hotel.
Even this functional shelter must have a 'Kerala touch'

As tourists, unmindful of such ironies, keep doing the semi-millennial walk, a small band of locals routinely chase a lot more modest heritage. A little legacy of music, built around a man who literally set the tone for the angst and mirth of subaltern Kochi. *Baayi* (brother) to his fans, Mehboob was a singer of popular songs, who could compose, improvise and transform. Across the lading named after Albuquerque in Calvetty, in a little chamber on top of a row of shops, his voice still resonates many years after his death.

Bismillah Abu and Husan Koya recalling Mehboob and his songs

As the sightseer's Kochi winds down by sundown, the first-floor fraternity comes alive. A few quiet men climb the once-carpeted wooden stairway and gather here to reminisce, rehearse and plan the next big do, to commemorate their icon. They are back from work, some from manual cargo handling at the port and the bazaar. The latter don't look any lowlier than the rest, all fit into that visually cohesive broad spectrum that Kerala calls middle class.

Mounted on a wall is a line-up of black and white photographs of yesteryear musicians with the odd atonal one in colour. You can't have too much order around. *Baayi* stood out, says a faithful. Never did any copycat singing. Never sang the same song twice; always surprised everyone. Wooden floors swept clean, a raised platform at one end shrouded in a creaseless white cloth and a dozen folding chairs and a table at the other, you wonder whether you have stepped into a prayer hall. After the daylong dosage of heritage, piety is hardly the thing you are looking for. The Spartan air is quickly relieved by easy laughter, banter, music and clouds of cigarette smoke.

'Kishore' Abu, another Mehboob loyalist

Next morning, as day breaks over the river beach dotted with Chinese nets, two veteran Mehboob loyalists, far too old to ascend the evening chamber's steps, turn up to sip tea, chat and break into song. Like muted notes from a hand-cranked gramophone, the voices rise and hold in the early morning stillness.

How long will this graying legacy last? Will it go on with a perennial half life? Or revive magically like the Buena Vista Social Club, the dwindling ensemble of ageing Cuban musicians brought to life by filmmaker Wim Wenders?

As Kochi wakes up to drown all music, a harbinger of great news stops by. An acquaintance of the singers, this trader of herbs has lately been on a purple patch. Just two months back he won Rs. 2 million in a lottery. This morning's news is even better. The make-or-break board exam results are out and his daughter has scored top marks.

For five weeks I saw, heard, sketched and read about nothing but the past, half a millennium of it. Finally, I sense some stirring of a future. The bright kid should go on to graduate, do well for herself and earn enough elsewhere to afford regular holidays back home. This is the familiar Kerala story.

Narendranath, a seller of herbs and country drugs

Even better, she might inherit daddy's good luck, come into big money, buy a beachside bungalow and play spoilsport. Refuse to sell out to the tourist operator and stay put. She would then be a singular tourist attraction, one who could call Fort Kochi her home, not homestay.

Thakur House, beachside residence of a family of tea planters and traders

Just what the visiting chronicler needs—a source other than fellow visitors. Fort Kochi will live as long as it has stories to tell the scribes who follow Santa Claus.

Graffiti artist Zubir, at one of his self-assigned wall spreads. He updates these moral, multi-religious epigrams from time to time

The islands off Fort Kochi and the mainland of Ernakulam

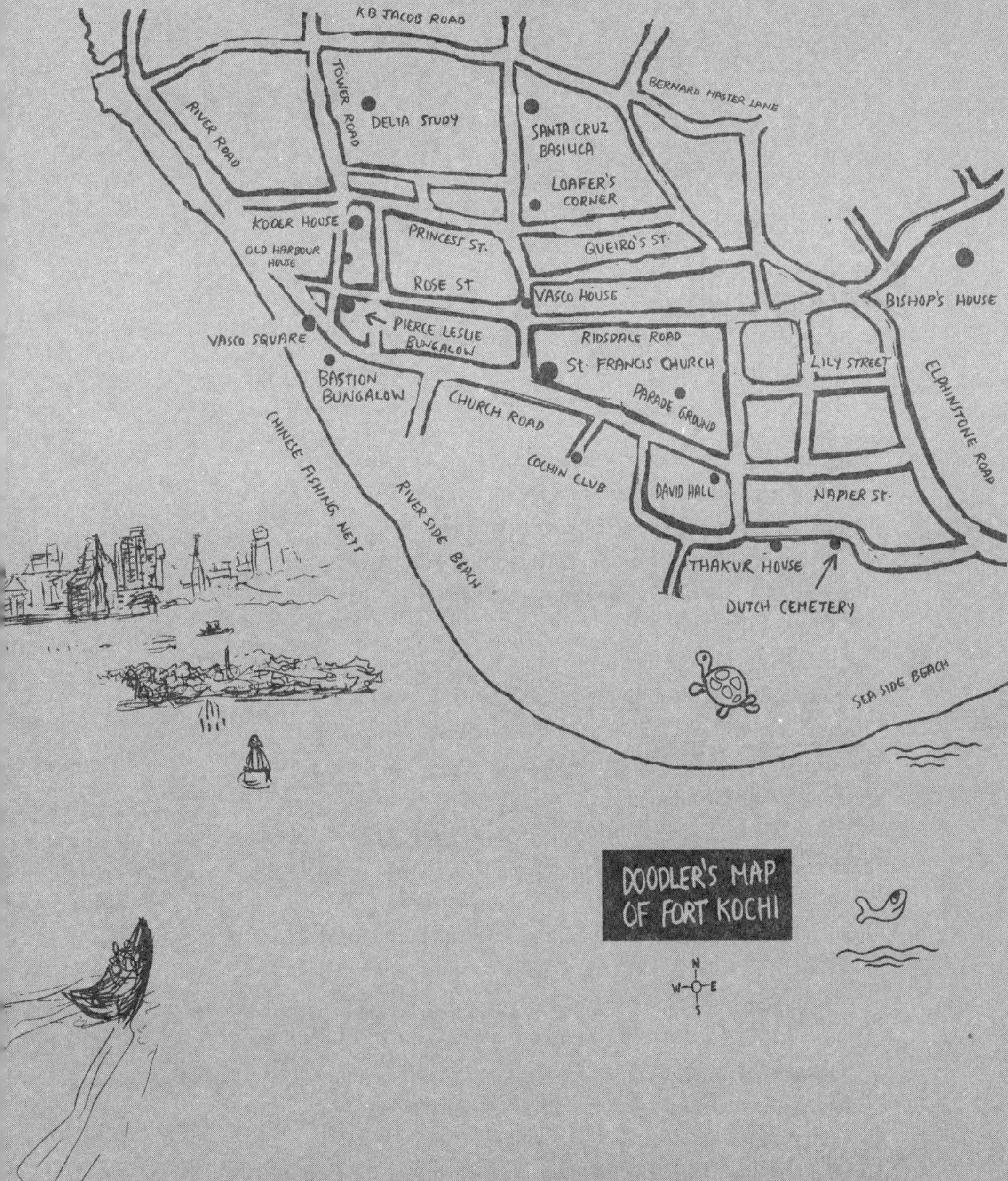
KB JACOB ROAD
BERNARD MASTER LANE
RIVER ROAD
TOWER ROAD
DELTA STUDY
SANTA CRUZ BASILICA
LOAFER'S CORNER
KODER HOUSE
OLD HARBOUR HOUSE
PRINCESS ST.
QUEIRO'S ST.
ROSE ST
VASCO HOUSE
BISHOP'S HOUSE
VASCO SQUARE
PIERCE LESLIE BUNGALOW
RIDSDALE ROAD
ST. FRANCIS CHURCH
LILY STREET
ELPHINSTONE ROAD
BASTION BUNGALOW
PARADE GROUND
CHURCH ROAD
COCHIN CLUB
DAVID HALL
NAPIER ST.
CHINESE FISHING NETS
RIVER SIDE BEACH
THAKUR HOUSE
DUTCH CEMETERY
SEA SIDE BEACH
DOODLER'S MAP OF FORT KOCHI
N
W
E
S

Bibliography

Baig, Amita & Henderson William, Facets of a Hundred Years Planting, Munnar, Kerala, Tata Finlay Limited, 1978.

Batuta, Ibn, Translated by Panikkassery Velayudhan, Keralam Arunnuru Kollam Munpu, Kozhikode, Kerala, 2007.

Bernard, K.L., *Kerala and the Portuguese*, Fort Kochi, Bri-Dan Printers, 1993.

Bernard, K.L., History of Fort Cochin, Mattancherry, Cochin, Swaraj Printers, Year unmentioned.

Bristow, Sir Robert, Cochin Saga, Cochin, Paico Publishing House 1959.

Cottineau De Kloguen, Denis L, An Historical Sketch of Goa, New Delhi, Asian Educational Services, 1831, Reprint 1988.

Danvers, Frederick Charles, The Portuguese in India , New Delhi, Asian Educational Services, 1894, Reprint 1988.

Davies, F.S., Cochin, British & Indian, London, Simpkin, Marshall, Hamilton, Kent & Co. Ltd., George Kenneth at The Diocesan Press, Vepery, Madras , 1923.

Day Francis, The Land of the Perumals Or Cochin, Its Past and Its Present, New Delhi, Asian Educational Services, 1863, 1990.

Gopal Panikkar, T.K., Malabar and its Folk, New Delhi, Asian Educational Services, 1900 Reprint 1983.

Israel, Nejamin. J, The Jews of India, New Delhi, Mosaic Books, 1982.

Iyer, L.R. Ananthakrishna, Then Cochin Tribes and Castes, Madras, Higginbothom & Co, 1912.

Katz, Nathan & Goldberg, Ellen.S., Kashrut, Caste and Kabbalah, The Religious Life of the Jews of Cochin, New Delhi, Manohar Publishers & Distributors, 2005.

Kochi rajah's grant of rights and privileges to Jewish ancestor Joseph Rabban, Facsimile of the copper plates in Cochin Synagogue, Cochin, Essen Industries, 1968.

Lawson, Charles Allen, British and Native Cochin, New Delhi, Asian Educational Services, 1861, 2001.

Madan, K.D., Life and Travels of Vasco da Gama, New Delhi, Asian Educational Services, 1998.

Mathew, K.S., Indo-Portuguese Trade and the Fuggers of Germany, New Delhi, Manohar Publishers & Distributors, `1997.

Mayer, Adrian.C., Land and Society in Malabar, London, Oxford University Press, 1952.

Namboodiripad, E.M.S., Kerala, Society and Politics, An Historical Survey, New Delhi, National Book Agency Pvt. Ltd, 1967, Reprint 1984.

Narayan Rajan, Sampoorna Swaraj, The Story of Goa's Liberation Struggle 1928-1961, Panjim-Goa, The Directorate of Art and Culture, Government of Goa.

Oaten, E.F., European Travellers in India During the Fifteenth, Sixteenth and Seventeenth Centuries, New Delhi, Asian Educational Services, 1909, Reprint1991.

Ouwerkerk Louise, No Elephants for the Maharaja, New Delhi, Manohar Publishers & Distributors, 1994.

Panikkar, K.M. Malabar and the Portuguese, New Delhi, Voice of India, 1929, Reprint 1997.

Prasad, N.Devi, Fort Cochin & Mattancherry, A Monograph, New Delhi, The Indian National Trust for Art and Cultural Heritage, 1994.

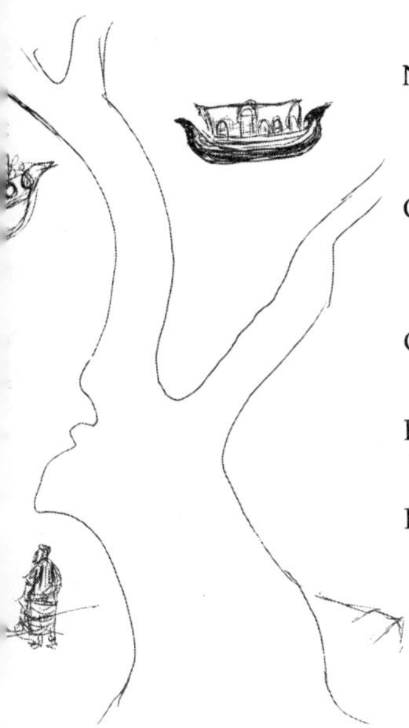

Priolkar, The Terrible Tribunal for the East, The Goa Inquisition, New Delhi, Voice of India, 1961.

Roth Joseph, The Wandering Jews, London, Granta Books, 2001.

Sanjay Subrahmanyam, The Career and Legend of Vasco da Gama, New Delhi, Foundation Books, Cambridge University Press, 1997.

Sanjay Subrahmanyam, The Political Economy of Commerce, Southern India 1500-1650, New Delhi, Foundation Books, Cambridge University Press, 2004.

Sarkar, H, Monuments of Kerala, New Delhi, Surya Print Process for Archaeological Survey of India, 1973, Reprint 1992.

Sethuram, P, Das, M.K., Venugopal, V.N., A Journey through Time 1857- 2007, Kottayam, India, DC Books, 2008.

Shastry, B.S., Studies in Indo-Portuguese History, Bangalore, IBH Prakashana Printery. 1981.

Stephens, H. Morse, Rulers of India, Albuquerque, New Delhi, Asian Educational Services, 1897, Reprint 2000.

Tampuran, Rama Varma (Appan), *Cochin*, Cochin, Published under the special authority of His Highness the Maharajah of Cochin. 1944.

Venn, L.W., Cochin-Malabar, Palms and Pageants, Cochin, Pierce Leslie and Co Ltd.

Whiteway, R.S., The Rise of Portuguese Power in India 1497-1550, New Delhi, Asian Educational Services, 1899. Reprint 1989.

Wood Conrad, The Moplah Rebellion and its Genesis, New Delhi, People's Publishing House, 1987.

Acknowledgements

Ashok Kumar, M.K. Das, Eapen Kalapurackal, Geeta Dharmarajan, S. Gopalakrishnan, Jose Dominic, N.S. Madhavan, P.K. Michael Tharakan, Nelson Fernandes, T.K. Prakash, Prem Nazir, Ravi Menon, Rizio Yohannan Raj, T.V.R. Shenoy, K.J. Sohan, C.R.R. Varma, V.N. Venugopal, G. Vijayaraghavan, Vimal Kumar G.